military supervision, the political maneuverings and economic ventures of such prominent figures as Joseph E. Brown, Benjamin Hill, and Hannibal I. Kimball, the efforts of the Ku-Klux Klan to nullify Negro voting rights and re-establish "white supremacy" concepts, and, finally, the investigations by the Democratic party of Republican misgovernment during the administration of Governor Rufus B. Bullock.

Dr. Conway, who did the research for the book in Georgia, has made considerable use of primary manuscripts, travelers' accounts, state and federal reports, and contemporary newspaper material to arrive at an account which judiciously assesses the claims and counterclaims of violently opposed groups which were vitally concerned with the place of the Negro in Southern society after emancipation and with the return of Georgia to the Union.

Alan Conway is a senior lecturer in American history at the University College of Wales, Aberystwyth, Wales. He is the editor of *The Welsh in America: Letters from the Immigrants.* (see back of jacket)

THE RECONSTRUCTION OF

GEORGIA

BY ALAN CONWAY

UNIVERSITY OF MINNESOTA PRESS
Minneapolis

Library of Congress Catalog Card Number: 66-18867

PUBLISHED IN GREAT BRITAIN, INDIA, AND PAKISTAN BY THE OXFORD
UNIVERSITY PRESS, LONDON, BOMBAY, AND KARACHI, AND IN CANADA BY
THE COPP CLARK PUBLISHING CO. LIMITED, TORONTO

PREFACE

I T I S somewhat surprising in view of the amount of revisionist work that has been done since the Second World War in the field of Reconstruction history that most of the studies of individual states during this period are anything up to half a century or more old. The two standard studies of Georgia, those of Woolley and of Miss Thompson, were written in 1901 and 1915 respectively. After fifty years, therefore, a new study of Georgia under the Reconstruction governments is not too premature. Some Americans may feel that it is a little presumptuous for an Englishman to tackle a job of this nature, particularly as the amount of time available for his basic research in Georgia itself has been limited to that provided by fellowships. Nevertheless, an attempt has been made to write a balanced account of a highly emotional subject. Distance from and non-involvement in the South are not necessarily virtues, but in this, the first state study of Reconstruction by anyone other than an American historian, the views of an outsider may prove of interest to students of the period. I do not agree with many of the opinions expressed by Miss Thompson, but the present study is in no way an attempt to denigrate what is a very good piece of work. Some sections of her *Reconstruction in Georgia* are admirable examples of meticulous research upon which it would be difficult to improve. No attempt, therefore, has been made to duplicate in detail what has already been adequately covered. It is largely on points of interpretation that we differ.

I am particularly indebted to the Rockefeller Foundation which through the British Association for American Studies made it possible for me to spend a year at Emory University in Atlanta, Georgia. My warmest thanks go to Dr. Harvey Young, the Chairman of the Department of History and to his colleagues at Emory for their unfailing courtesy, kindness and help to me; to Dr. Horace Montgomery at the University of Georgia, to Messrs. Erwin, Birchmore, and Epting for permission to use the Howell Cobb papers; to all those in Georgia who helped me to secure material for this study and particularly to the library staffs at Emory University, at the University of Georgia in Athens, and at Columbia University. My greatest debt is to Dr. James C. Bonner of the Woman's College of Georgia, Milledgeville, who most generously made available to me the results of his own researches. Finally, I would like to express my thanks to my own college at Aberystwyth for granting me leave of absence to work in Georgia and to Mrs. Sîan Hayward and Mrs. Carol O'Toole who typed and retyped the manuscript.

ALAN CONWAY

Aberystwyth
September 1965

TABLE OF CONTENTS

The Reconstruction of Georgia

I

THE LATTER DAYS

GEORGIA, deep in the heart of the Confederacy, was fortunate in that apart from a few months between the spring of 1864 and the end of the year, no armed forces fought over her soil. In January 1861, Governor Joseph E. Brown had, as a precautionary measure, taken possession of Fort Pulaski which defended Savannah, then the largest and most important city in the state, with a population of almost fourteen thousand whites and eight thousand colored people.[1] Georgia held on to Fort Pulaski until April 1862 when the garrison of four hundred men was forced to surrender to Federal troops. All attempts by Union forces to take Fort McAllister on the Ogeechee river were, however, beaten off and activity in the Savannah area was limited largely to raids on plantations on the sea islands and on the coast and to the burning of Darien in 1863.[2]

Only on two further occasions before 1864 was the war brought home to the state; both of these were closely connected with attempts by Federal forces to destroy the state-owned Western and Atlantic Railroad as an effective supply line for the Confederate forces operating in Tennessee. The first attempt was made in April 1862. James J. Andrews with twenty-one picked men in civilian clothes penetrated to a point on the road just north of Atlanta where they seized an unattended

---

1 J. C. Bonner, *The Georgia Story* (Harlow Publishing Corporation, Oklahoma City–Chattanooga, 1958), p. 286. *U.S. Census, 1860*, p. 74, Table no. 3.
2 Bonner, p. 286.

locomotive. Heading northward, they proceeded to pull up the track behind them, burn bridges, and cut telegraph wires. Hotly pursued by Captain William A. Fuller, a railroad conductor, and a number of volunteers, Andrews and his men eventually ran out of fuel and had to abandon the engine near Ringgold, close to the Tennessee border. Andrews and seven others were captured, court-martialed, and hanged as spies. Very little real damage had been done to the road, but Governor Brown quickly realized that effective measures had to be taken to safeguard this vital link in Confederate railroad communications.

The second strike against the Western and Atlantic Railroad was much more orthodox and even less successful. In the spring of 1863, Colonel Abel D. Streight with a cavalry force of fifteen hundred crossed into Georgia from Alabama intending to cut the line and prevent supplies' being sent to General Braxton Bragg through Chattanooga. Repulsed at Rome near the Coosa river in northwestern Georgia and harried by Confederate cavalry under General Nathan B. Forrest, Streight retreated to Cedar Bluff in Alabama where he was forced to surrender in May 1863.[3]

Thus, before 1864 Georgia experienced little more than the odd foray and a flurry of excitement caused by Andrews's raiders. At the end of 1863, however, a cloud much larger than a man's hand appeared which would forever mar the serenity of Georgia. On September 9, 1863, the Confederate forces under Braxton Bragg surrendered Chattanooga just north of the Georgia line to General Rosecrans. Initially, this evacuation did not seem to be a major disaster because ten days later at the ferocious battle of Chickamauga, the Federal forces were heavily defeated, forced to retreat to Chattanooga, and saved from complete destruction only by the efforts of General George H. Thomas, "the Rock of Chickamauga." The position of the Federal forces seemed to be desperate. Besieged in Chattanooga, short of food and supplies, with the Confederate forces controlling the railroads entering Chattanooga and occupying the strategic heights of Missionary Ridge and Lookout Mountain overlooking the town, it seemed possible that they would either be starved into surrender or forced to evacuate the town. The situation changed drastically, however, with Rosecrans being superseded by Thomas as commander of the Army of the Cumberland and with Grant being raised to supreme command of Union operations in the West.[4] Grant swiftly began to strengthen his forces; between November 23 and

November 25, 1863, Bragg's forces were shattered at the battle of Lookout Mountain–Missionary Ridge. Chattanooga was relieved, the Confederate forces retreated to Dalton, Georgia, and the state for the first time found herself facing the prospect of an attack in strength. General William T. Sherman was given the task of moving against Atlanta, but the presence of General Joseph E. Johnston, a master of defensive generalship who had replaced Bragg, with more than fifty thousand men at Dalton, ensured that Sherman's advance was not likely to be a simple military promenade into the center of Georgia. Although Sherman had over ninety thousand men at Chattanooga, his long lines of railroad communications extending some five hundred miles to Louisville were shaky and vulnerable to guerilla raids. Moreover, the rough country over which he would be operating made the movement of this number of troops a matter of considerable difficulty. Sherman moved from Chattanooga at the beginning of May 1864 and Johnston had little hope that with the forces at his command he could halt Sherman's advance. What he could do, however, was to make it excessively expensive by avoiding any commitment to a major trial of strength, by always fighting from prepared entrenchments of his own choosing, by retreating slowly behind destroyed bridges and railroad track until he could back into Atlanta's fortifications with his fighting strength relatively unimpaired. Sherman was checked at the battles of Resaca on May 13–16 and New Hope Church on May 25–28, suffering severe losses. From New Hope Church, Sherman swung back toward the Western and Atlantic Railroad, only to find Johnston blocking his way south on the lower slopes of Kennesaw Mountain. Sherman attacked the well-entrenched Confederate troops and was thrown back with heavy losses. It was, however, but a temporary check. In the next three weeks, a tactical battle of thrust and parry took place between the two commanders which brought the Federal forces ever closer to Atlanta. By the beginning of July, Johnston was no longer able to hold the line of the Chattahoochee river and retreated to the partially built trenches around Atlanta. By July 10 Sherman was across the Chattahoochee and Johnston was forced back to the ring of prepared fortifications on the immediate outskirts of the city. Discontent with the Fabian tactics of

---

3   Bonner, p. 288.
4   Despite violent criticism of Bragg's handling of operations by many of his subordinate generals, he was retained in command by Jefferson Davis.

Johnston welled up; the desire to see Sherman thrown neck and crop out of Georgia overcame sound judgment and on July 17 Johnston was relieved of his command on orders from the Confederate government at Richmond and replaced by a thirty-three-year-old, one-legged, battle-scarred veteran of Gettysburg and Chickamauga, General John B. Hood. As expected, Hood took the offensive and fought two expensive battles, the first on July 20 at Peachtree Creek and the second the battle of Atlanta on July 22. Hood's strategy was blighted by ill timing and bad luck, and he found himself back in the trenches before Atlanta unable to prevent Sherman from cutting the city's railroad communications and commencing a month-long siege. The bombardment of Atlanta went on for over a month, until August 25 when Sherman swung a considerable force south of the city and struck at the Central of Georgia Railroad coming from Macon. This move put Hood in the very position in which he had hoped to place Sherman, that of being isolated with his supply lines cut. A Confederate attack at Jonesboro on August 31 was easily repulsed and Hood decided to evacuate the city on the night of September 1–2 with some forty thousand of his troops intact. Instead of trying to block any further advance into Georgia, Hood subsequently struck confidently toward Tennessee and Sherman's long communications to the rear, firm in the belief that Sherman would have no alternative in the face of such a threat but to retrace his steps.[5]

Meanwhile, Sherman took what in effect was the first step in the reconstruction of Georgia. In mid-September 1864 the well-known Georgia Unionist Joshua Hill sought permission from the general to recover the body of his son who had been killed somewhere near Cassville as the Southern armies retreated. Sherman, well aware that Unionist sentiment in Georgia was far from negligible, took the opportunity to invite Governor Brown, through Hill, to visit him with a view to Georgia's withdrawing her forces from the Confederate armies and, in effect, concluding a separate peace. In return for such a measure, he was prepared to spare the state further devastation by keeping his troops to the main roads and paying for all the corn and food he required. Similar messages were sent through Judge Wright of Rome, a former member of Congress, and William King of Marietta.[6] Sherman's suggestion was not entirely outrageous. Already on September 10 Brown had issued an executive order from Milledgeville, the capital of Georgia, withdrawing the state militia from Hood's Army of the Tennessee on the grounds that the militia had been called for service only in the defense of Atlanta and that they were now needed on their own land to harvest corn and sorghum.[7] Brown's reasons for the withdrawal of the Georgia militia were somewhat flimsy but in keeping with his attitude toward the Confederate government of Jefferson Davis throughout the war. The governor of Georgia considered that the interests of the state were paramount over those of the Confederacy as a whole. But a step of such magnitude as that of concluding a separate peace was not to be taken lightly even if he could get the support of someone like Alexander H. Stephens, the Georgian vice-president of the Confederacy. Such support was unlikely to be forthcoming, despite Stephens' known unionism and loyalty to Georgia. Brown was sufficient of a realist to recognize that Georgia could be saved from much suffering and despoliation by accepting Sherman's terms. He was a man who lacked neither courage nor foresight and, as his subsequent career would show, did not hesitate to advocate measures which were temporarily unpopular but ultimately fruitful. But at this stage it was not impossible that Sherman might, as Jefferson Davis bravely asserted, be forced to retreat from Atlanta like Napoleon from Moscow half a century earlier.[8] In addition, Lincoln's re-election to the presidency at the end of 1864 was by no means certain and a negotiated peace, tantamount to a Southern victory, should the Democrats elect General George B. McClellan, was not beyond the bounds of possibility. To have guessed incorrectly at this juncture could have been fatal for Brown as a Southerner, as a politician, and as a businessman, but the governor possessed the almost uncanny ability always to be on both ends of the political see-saw at the same time. In a public statement rejecting Sherman's offer he stressed that although Georgia had the sovereign right to act independently if she so wished, she had pledged her faith to the South and that pledge would not be violated. He concluded, however, with a strong hint to the Confederate government that it was high time

---

5 For good accounts of this phase of operations see Bonner, pp. 290–295. J. G. Randall and David Donald, *The Civil War and Reconstruction*, 2nd ed. (Boston, 1961), pp. 412–416, 424–426. *Official Records of the War of the Rebellion* . . . (Washington, 1897), Series I, Vol. XXXVIII, pt. 1, pp. 61–85.

6 W. T. Sherman, *Memoirs of Gen. W. T. Sherman* (New York, 1891), Vol. II, pp. 137–138.

7 *Ibid.*, pp. 138–139.

8 *Ibid.*, p. 141.

for the war to be brought to an end and further pointless bloodshed avoided.[9] Brown was thus able very deftly to proclaim himself loyal to the South and fighting to the end while at the same time demonstrating his concern for Georgia and the need for peace. Whatever the outcome of the struggle, Brown had taken out a completely valid policy of political insurance.

Brown's decision left Sherman no other alternative but to carry out his threat to devastate Georgia. One thing was certain and that was that Atlanta would be destroyed once his forces left the city either in pursuit of Hood northwards or on the march to the sea. Simply to remain at Atlanta was an open invitation to complete destruction. The fate of the city was thus in no doubt in Sherman's mind from the moment of occupation. His order for the evacuation of the city by the civilian population prior to its destruction resulted in some bitter correspondence with Hood who, unable to grasp Sherman's twentieth-century concept of total war, denounced him for his barbarity and inhumanity.[10] Sherman's concern for the plight of the civilian population would seem to have been genuine. He was prepared to provide food and transportation for them wherever they chose to go, north or south, but they could not be allowed to remain in Atlanta where their very presence could hamper the mobility of the Union forces. It was not a pleasant decision that Sherman took and it was made no easier by the reports that he received from escapees of the revolting conditions under which twenty-five thousand Federal prisoners were living in the notorious Andersonville military stockade-prison in south Georgia where scores of men were dying miserably for want of food and rudimentary medical care.[11]

Of greater significance for the ultimate outcome of the war was the question whether to retrace his steps and deal with Hood before venturing further into Georgia or whether to leave General George H. Thomas the task of containing Hood with a smaller force, cut his communications completely with the north, and march across Georgia to Savannah relying upon foraging to sustain his forces. The boldness of the latter step left Lincoln (as he subsequently admitted to Sherman) "anxious, if not fearful,"[12] but the president wisely refrained from interfering and left the decision to Grant. Finally, on November 2, 1864, Sherman received the vital dispatch from Grant which gave approval for the march to the sea. "I do not really see that you can withdraw from where you are to follow Hood without giving up all we have gained in territory. I say, then, go as you propose." [13]

The huge amounts of stores which had accumulated at Atlanta were sent with the sick by railroad northward, and on November 12 all railroad and telegraph communications to the rear were severed leaving the army dependent entirely upon its own resources and supplies.[14] By November 14 all available troops consisting of 55,329 infantry, 5,063 cavalry, and 1,812 artillery had assembled at or near Atlanta.[15] These troops were supplied with about 2,500 wagons loaded with ammunition and provisions. Bread for twenty days, sugar and coffee for forty days, and a double allowance of salt for forty days were considered very much as emergency rations. All else that was needed would have to come from the countryside on the line of march. Something like 5,000 head of cattle were driven along on the hoof, but so successful were the foraging parties that on arrival at Savannah this number had risen to 10,000.[16] Ammunition being in comparatively short supply, orders were issued that the greatest possible economy in its use was to be practiced.[17]

Before the march from Atlanta began on the morning of November 15 the engineers leveled and then set fire to the depot, roundhouse, and machine shops of the Georgia Railroad. The fires that were set were not kept under control and spread widely in the heart of the city.[18] How extensive was the damage by fire to Atlanta remains a matter of some doubt. One Georgia historian maintains that "nearly all the city was engulfed in flames from burning warehouses, factories and ordnance stores." [19] Sidney Andrews, the correspondent of the Boston *Advertiser* and the Chicago *Tribune*, writing from Atlanta on November 23, 1865, pointed out with rather wry humor, "Atlanta . . . excepting Boston is the most irregularly laid out city I ever saw. In fact the greater portion

9   C. Mildred Thompson, *Reconstruction in Georgia* (Columbia University Press, 1915), p. 38.
10   Sherman, II, pp. 118–124.
11   *Ibid.*, p. 143.
12   *Official Records*, Series I, Vol. XLIV, p. 809.
13   *Ibid.*, Series I, Vol. XXXIX, pt. 3, p. 594.
14   *Ibid.*, pp. 740–741, 762–764.
15   *Ibid.*, Series I, Vol. XLIV, p. 16.
16   *Ibid.*, pp. 8, 726.
17   *Ibid.*, p. 452.
18   Sherman, II, p. 177.
19   Bonner, p. 295.

of it seems never to have been laid out at all till Sherman's army came in here."[20] Andrews, before he reached Atlanta, was under the impression that it had been totally destroyed. On examination, however, he found that the whole of the business section had been laid in ruins with the exception of the Masonic Hall and one block of six stores and a hotel. Large residences in all parts of the city had been damaged or destroyed but the city hall, all the churches, and most of the houses of the middle and poorer classes had been spared.[21]

One report sent to Governor Brown by General W. P. Howard listed all transportation together with car sheds, depots, machine shops, foundries, rolling mills, and arsenal as being destroyed. The jail was burned, as were many business houses and private homes around the city hall. He estimated that three thousand houses were destroyed in the center and two thousand further out.[22] An interesting comment on the mores of the times was that on arrival at Atlanta he found about 250 wagons belonging to bushwhackers, deserters, and country folk who had descended upon the city and were busily engaged upon the task of carrying off everything they could lay their hands on.[23]

There could be no doubt, however, that Sherman had left his mark on Atlanta and served notice upon Georgians generally that he was imposing a new concept of war upon them, a concept which might not measure up to traditional standards of chivalry but which was thorough and effective. Sherman left Atlanta with its ruined buildings still on fire and black smoke rising high in the clear air and hanging like a dirty shroud over the city. In contrast, the white-topped supply wagons stretched away in a long line toward the south; gun barrels glistened in the bright sunshine and the troops were in fine fettle, a devil-may-care feeling pervading all ranks.[24] Sherman's primary aim was to place his army in the very heart of Georgia between Macon and Augusta. As a result, Confederate forces would have to be divided in order to defend those points and also Millen and Savannah, and Charleston, South Carolina.[25] To achieve this aim most effectively, the army was divided into two wings. The right wing, commanded by Major-General Oliver O. Howard (later to be head of the Freedmen's Bureau), moved through Jonesboro and Monticello toward Macon before swinging eastward to Gordon and Irwinton. The left wing under Major-General H. W. Slocum headed for the first objective, Milledgeville, by way of Covington, Madison, and Eatonton.[26] Brigadier-General Judson Kilpatrick, in command of the cavalry, was ordered first to move on the right of the Army of the Tennessee (the right wing) toward Macon, striking the railroad as near Macon as possible, then to fall back toward Gordon destroying railroad track, and finally to join up with Sherman at Milledgeville within one week.[27]

Sherman himself marched parallel with Slocum and his first-night camp by the roadside near Lithonia set the pattern of his advance. The great granite mass of Stone Mountain was outlined clearly in the light of hundreds of bonfires of railroad ties upon which ripped-up rails were heated and then bent into ingenious shapes around treetrunks. This destruction of railroad track was given the close personal attention of Sherman himself throughout the campaign.[28]

The extent and, more important, the intent of the activities of Sherman's foraging parties on the march to Savannah remain a matter of some controversy. In his Special Field Order No. 120 issued to his commanders before leaving Atlanta, Sherman laid it down quite clearly that brigade commanders were responsible for organizing foraging parties under the command of one or more "discreet officers" which would gather up corn, meat, vegetables, cornmeal, or whatever was needed by the command. The soldiers were forbidden to enter dwelling houses but were permitted when halted or in camp to take turnips, potatoes, and other vegetables and to drive in stock in sight of their camp. The gathering of provisions and forage at any distance from the line of march was entrusted only to regular foraging parties. Corps commanders only were given the power to destroy mills, houses, cotton gins, and the like, and only then in areas where bushwhacker or guerilla activity was encountered. How far such destruction should be punitive was left to the discretion of the corps commanders. Horses, mules, and wagons could be taken by the cavalry and artillery without limit, although preferably from the rich who were likely to be hostile rather than from the poor who were more likely to be neutral or friendly.

---

20 Sidney Andrews, *The South since the War* (Boston, 1866), p. 338.
21 *Ibid.*, p. 339.
22 Townsend Collection, Vol. 52, no. 197.
23 *Ibid.*
24 Sherman, II, pp. 178–179.
25 *Official Records*, Series I, Vol. XLIV, p. 8.
26 *Ibid.*, Series I, Vol. XLIV, p. 8; Vol. XXXIX, pt. 3, p. 713.
27 *Ibid.*, Series I, Vol. XLIV, p. 362.
28 Sherman, II, pp. 180–181.

Some mules and horses could be taken by regiments or brigades to replace jaded animals. Able-bodied Negroes could be taken along by the armies and organized into pioneer battalions provided that supplies in addition to those needed for the soldiers were adequate. Finally and somewhat optimistically Sherman forbade "abusive or threatening language" being used to the inhabitants of Georgia.[29]

Unfortunately for those Georgians who lived on or near the line of march these instructions were easier to put on paper than into force. It was impossible to check a great deal of unauthorized foraging, and much pillaging, plundering, looting, and violence undoubtedly took place. The only commander who seemed to have been unduly disturbed about this was Major-General Howard, who issued a field order that any officer or man of his command who was discovered pillaging or burning property without authority would be shot.[30] Once again, this was an order that had more bark than bite. From the reports of subordinate commanders it is quite clear that there was no shortage of food in Georgia at this time. There was evidence of much wealth among the inhabitants along the line of march, and the troops found an abundance of corn, beef, mutton, sweet potatoes, poultry, molasses, and honey.[31] The work of the foraging parties was thus made all too easy. So much was brought in each day with so little effort that on striking camp each morning the troops preferred to leave behind what had not been used rather than carry these supplies with them. The result was wanton waste and foraging which was closer to pillaging than the supplying of genuine need.[32]

The Confederate forces were powerless to hinder the advance or to prevent the rape of the rich countryside. Some of Hood's cavalry detachments under Major-General Joseph Wheeler tried to harass Sherman's forces, but to little effect. A small, motley battalion composed of convicts from the penitentiary and cadets from the Georgia Military Institute, including Governor Brown's sixteen-year-old son, was assembled at Milledgeville, but was roughly handled at an engagement on the Oconee river. Around Macon some three thousand state troops consisting of old men and boys were commanded by Generals G. W. Smith and Howell Cobb, and General William J. Hardee had got together a nondescript force of about ten thousand to defend Savannah.[33] For all practical purposes, the opposition which could be offered to Sherman's advance was negligible. The greater threat to the fighting efficiency of the armies was the number of horses so easily available. Too many of the infantry became part-time cavalry and as a result Sherman ordered large numbers of horses to be shot to stop the disorganizing effect of ill-controlled mounted infantry.[34]

Milledgeville was taken on November 23, Governor Brown, the state officers, and the legislature having already left the capital. In their absence some of Sherman's officers formed themselves into a mock legislature in the hall of representatives and repealed the ordinance of secession.[35] Less lightheartedly, the railroad depot, two arsenals, a powder magazine, and other public buildings and shops were burned. The railroad track for five miles toward Gordon was torn up; twenty-three hundred muskets, ten thousand cartridges, five thousand lances, and fifteen hundred cutlasses were burned; and a hundred and seventy boxes of artillery ammunition, two hundred kegs of powder, and sixteen hogsheads of salt were thrown into the river. About eighteen hundred bales of cotton were disposed of by Sherman and fifteen hundred pounds of tobacco were distributed among the troops.[36]

From Milledgeville the two wings of the army converged on Sandersville and continued the advance toward Savannah by way of Louisville and Millen. The Union forces reached the coast on December 12, captured Fort McAllister, and besieged Savannah. Resistance lasted little more than a week and on December 21 the city was abandoned as General Hardee withdrew his troops across the Savannah river into South Carolina.[37] Lincoln's Christmas present from Sherman included a hundred and fifty heavy guns, thirteen locomotives, a hundred and ninety cars, three steamers, and thirty-two thousand bales of cotton.[38] Hardee was unable to prevent the capture of this rich hoard of cotton by the Federal forces. He could not burn it before he left the city because it was stored in cellars, garrets, and warehouses throughout the city where it could not be burned without endangering the homes

29   *Official Records*, Series I, Vol. XXXIX, pt. 3, pp. 713–714.
30   *Ibid.*, Series I, Vol. XLIV, p. 521.
31   *Ibid.*, p. 267.
32   *Ibid.*, pp. 177, 178.
33   Bonner, pp. 296, 298; Sherman, II, p. 188.
34   *Official Records*, Series I, Vol. XLIV, p. 727.
35   Sherman, II, p. 190.
36   *Official Records*, Series I, Vol. XLIV, pp. 207, 249.
37   *Ibid.*, pp. 8–13, 737–738.
38   *Ibid.*, p. 786.

of the inhabitants. It could not be removed by rail before the road was cut because the removal of ordnance and army supplies took priority. It could not be removed by road because every dray and wagon was needed to keep the troops supplied with adequate food and ammunition.[39]

To Sherman the march to the sea was relatively unimportant when compared with his intended march into South Carolina and the final strangulation of the Confederacy. To him the prime necessity was to shift the base of his operations from Atlanta to Savannah,[40] but the unexpected ferocity and swiftness of this part of the campaign were decisive factors in breaking down Southern hopes and Southern morale. The fifty-mile wide weal that Sherman lashed across the face of Georgia was a reminder to Georgians not only of the cost of war but also of the cost of failing to make terms when they were offered. Sherman estimated the damage to the state of Georgia as $100,000,000 of which $80,000,000 was simple waste and destruction.[41] Howard's estimates were 3,523 bales of cotton burned, 9,000 head of cattle eaten, 931 horses and 1,850 mules captured, 4,500,000 pounds of corn and the same amount of fodder taken from the countryside, 191 miles of railroad destroyed, and about 3,000 Negroes set free.[42] Slocum's estimates were even more startling. He reported that his troops took from the countryside 919,000 rations of bread, 1,217,527 rations of meat, 483,000 rations of coffee, 581,534 rations of sugar, 1,146,500 rations of soap, and 137,000 rations of salt; 4,090 horses and mules were captured, together with 5,000,000 pounds of grain and 6,000,000 pounds of fodder; 119 miles of railroad track were torn up and machine shops, turntables, depots, and water tanks at Rutledge, Madison, Eatonton, Milledgeville, Tennville, and Davisborough were destroyed; 17,000 bales of cotton were destroyed, and a large number of cotton gins and presses; about 14,000 Negroes of all ages joined his columns, about half of whom reached the coast with him.[43] Kilpatrick's contribution to the grand total of destruction was the burning of 14,000 bales of cotton, 12,900 bushels of corn, 80 tons of fodder, 36 grist mills, 27 sawmills, and 271 cotton gins.[44] Even allowing for exaggerated claims and the relatively restricted area in which these operations had taken place, Sherman's march from Atlanta to Savannah was a savage blow to Georgia. The feverish pleas of Southern and Georgian leaders for Sherman's army to be utterly destroyed[45] were shown to be so much whistling in the darkness of defeat. To many Georgians, indeed, the fall of Savannah was a relief.[46]

Some two hundred people from Savannah were provided with transportation to Charleston, mostly families of those serving in the Confederate armies, but the bulk of the city's twenty thousand inhabitants chose to remain. The mayor and city council, strictly subordinate to the military, were restored to control over civic affairs and reasonable relations were established between the people and the army.[47]

Major-General J. W. Geary was put in command of Savannah and soon established markets for provisions, meat, and wood. For those destitute families lacking the money necessary to buy provisions the army provided food from its own stores. A large warehouse of rice was entrusted to a number of citizens who went to Boston and returned with shipments of flour, hams, sugar, and coffee which were distributed free to relieve those most in need.[48] Over a thousand loaves collected for the army were also turned over to the Poor Association of Savannah.[49]

Meanwhile, relief agencies in the North had been particularly concerned with the plight of Savannah. There was some opposition in the New York Chamber of Commerce to fattening rebels with relief, but

---

39 *Ibid.*, Vol. XLVII, pt. 2, p. 1105.
40 Sherman, II, p. 221.
41 *Official Records*, Series I, Vol. XLIV, p. 13.
42 *Ibid.*, p. 76.
43 *Ibid.*, p. 159. It is interesting to note in this context that some criticism came from Washington of Sherman's failure to strip Georgia of her Negroes by allowing a great many more to accompany his forces to the sea. It was felt that his action in burning bridges behind him prevented large numbers of Negroes from fleeing and left them to the mercy of their owners. *Ibid.*, p. 836. Sherman, in his reply to Halleck who had informed him of these views held by some people close to the president, made it quite clear that if his forces had been overburdened with too many Negroes, many of them women and children, the whole campaign could have been jeopardized had he encountered the enemy in strength. In typical Sherman fashion he stated, "Thank God, I am not running for an office and am not concerned because the rising generation will believe that I burned 500 niggers at one pop in Atlanta, or any such nonsense. The South deserves all she has got for her injustice to the negro, but that is no reason why we should go to the other extreme." *Ibid.*, Vol. XLVII, pt. 2, pp. 36–37.
44 *Ibid.*, Vol. XLIV, pp. 366–367.
45 *Ibid.*, p. 867.
46 *Ibid.*, p. 817.
47 *Ibid.*, pp. 812, 817. Sherman, II, pp. 234–235.
48 Sherman, II, pp. 236–237.
49 New York *World*, January 13, 1865, quoting Augusta *Chronicle and Sentinel*, January 4, 1865.

many members were at pains to point out that providing relief for the South would go much further toward recreating a spirit of union than all the armed forces.[50] Merchants met together in Philadelphia and in Faneuil Hall, Boston, to consider the best means of sending supplies to Savannah and by mid-January 1865 the Boston relief fund had reached $30,000.[51] On January 9, 1865, Edward Everett, the celebrated Massachusetts orator, made one of the last speeches of his life in Boston in favor of the Savannah Aid Scheme.[52] The earlier opposition in New York soon faded and the *Rebecca Clyde*, supplied by the New York and Washington Steamship Company, was loaded with seventeen hundred barrels of flour, salt meat, beans, bread, and a few luxuries, while $40,000 worth of provisions were put aboard the *Daniel Webster*, which was supplied by the government.[53]

On the arrival of these vessels at Savannah, the members of the New York committee met with a citizens' committee of one member from each ward to set up a system of issuing tickets to those whom they considered to be in need of relief. Distribution took place at the public market to whites and colored people alike, although it was noted that the greater portion of those receiving relief were in fact colored.[54] Many of these colored recipients of relief in return gave their labor at the barracks, military offices, and wharves.[55] In the same month an appeal was made to Northerners on behalf of the freedmen of Georgia for shoes and clothes, particularly for women and children, as they were unable to wear cast-off soldiers' clothing.[56] The army was success-ful in maintaining good order in the city. Soldiers were not allowed to enter private residences and the custom house and post office were cleaned out and made ready for a resumption of business. The Negroes, for the most part, were orderly and quiet, many of them remaining with their former owners. A store was opened to sell provisions brought in from the North, and greenbacks for this purpose were put into circula-tion. Early in January a correspondent of the New York *World* reported that Union sentiment in Georgia, although not active, might declare itself if repercussions from Richmond were not likely to be felt. His opinion was that Georgia was better disposed than any other part of the South toward the federal government.[57] Not unnaturally, Union sentiment in Georgia was divided. Some were in favor of immediate cooperation and reunion, others preferred to await the final outcome of the war.[58] By February 1865 Union meetings were being held in Savannah which reflected strong peace sentiments from some nineteen counties, particularly noticeable being the northwestern counties but central and southeast Georgia too, it was claimed, had large numbers who were eager to return to the Union.[59] In March, the New York *Daily Tribune* went so far as to publish a list of prominent Georgians, who, it alleged, were in favor of reconstruction on the basis of the Union and the Constitution. Among those named were Herschel V. Johnson, Benjamin H. Hill, Joseph E. Brown, Joshua Hill, and Judge Linton Stephens (Alexander H. Stephens's half-brother).[60] For the most part, however, the early months of 1865 were months of indecision and, except for some activity at the docks in Savannah where government supplies were being unloaded and cotton and rice being shipped, as one observer put it, "The potent spell of poverty, idleness and a singular lethargy broods over everything. Groups of citizens could be seen some in the dirty grey of the rebel army, others in the coarse butternut colored cloth of country manufacture and still others in dilapidated old-fashioned garments, thread-bare and glossy — recalling better days." [61] Sherman had no intention of remaining very long in Savannah, because he was anxious to continue his march into South Carolina. So on January 18, 1865, Slocum was ordered to turn over the city to General J. G. Foster

---

50   New York *Herald,* January 7, 1865.
51   Townsend Collection, Vol. 52, nos. 139, 153, 204.
52   New York *Herald,* January 10, 1865.
53   Townsend Collection, Vol. 52, no. 227.
54   *Ibid.,* Vol. 52, no. 454.
55   New York *World,* January 21, 1865.
56   *Freedmen's Record,* I, no. 2, pp. 26–27.
57   New York *World,* January 14, 1865. It is worth noting in this context that among the mountain people of north Georgia support for the Confederacy had never been strong and defection and desertion were common. Unionist sentiment in Pickens county was so strong that the flag of the United States continued to be flown for several weeks after secession had taken place. Governor Brown, who understood these people well, refused to take drastic action against them. Bonner, p. 302.
58   New York *World,* January 31, 1865.
59   Townsend Collection, Vol. 53, no. 24. For a good example of instant cooperation see *Official Records,* Series I, Vol. XLIV, pp. 827–828.
60   New York *Daily Tribune,* March 25, 1865. Conspicuously absent are the names of the great Georgian triumvirate, Robert Toombs, Howell Cobb, and Alexander H. Stephens, although Stephens was a stronger Unionist than many of his contemporaries.
61   Townsend Collection, Vol. 53, no. 263.

and three days later Sherman departed for the final assault on Richmond and the complete strangulation of the Confederacy.[62]

Foster's task was no easy one. The health of the city was not very good. Large numbers of dead horses, mules, and cattle remained lying about and the offal from the cattle slaughtered to feed the troops did not improve the sanitary condition of the city. Smallpox was very prevalent among the Negroes who came crowding in from all parts of the state and vaccination went ahead apace, local doctors working closely with their military counterparts.[63] A shortage of fuel also continued to be a problem for some weeks and some citizens were reduced to burning fences and even furniture to keep themselves warm. Speculators, seeing their opportunity, made large and quick profits on the sale of fuel despite the efforts of a Fuel Committee to bring in supplies at the controlled price of $6 a cord for pine wood and $10 a cord for oak. Some fifty cords were distributed free to the destitute, but it was hoped that the situation would be relieved somewhat by the arrival of three hundred tons of coal that was expected from the North.[64]

The last act of defiance in Savannah occurred a week after Sherman's departure when the naval magazine (with fifty tons of powder and several hundred shells) was blown up. Fires broke out, destroying some two hundred houses or so in the third district.[65] This outrage, attributed to the Confederates, was little more than an empty gesture. With the fall of Savannah the war was virtually over as far as Georgia was concerned. Her troops continued to fight with the Confederate forces and officially Georgia did not capitulate until April 30, 1865, when Governor Brown surrendered the Georgia troops to General James H. Wilson who had occupied Macon shortly before Lee's surrender. Federal forces proceeded to take possession of Augusta and reoccupied Milledgeville and Atlanta and garrisons were established from which central points the state could be controlled.[66]

The key figure in this period of doubt and indecision, as would be the case in later years, was Governor Brown, who wrote from Augusta on April 25, 1865, to Alexander H. Stephens,

I am now remaining here to learn the result of the conference going on under the armistice. When that is announced I will try to shape my course as best I can. I have made up my mind to remain in the State,[67] and do all I can to aid in the restoration of order and to mitigate suffering as long as I am allowed to do so. If I am arrested and carried off, I have prepared my mind to meet my fate with coolness.[68]

Brown was not without courage: maintaining that destitution and the collapse of the currency made it essential for the state legislature to meet, he called for its assembly on May 22, 1865. General J. H. Wilson promptly forbade this and informed both Edwin M. Stanton, Secretary of War, and General J. M. Schofield of his decision asserting that he could see "no necessity for conventions at best and certainly not when controlled by prominent secessionists." [69] Brown appealed over the head of Wilson and his immediate superiors to President Andrew Johnson and the latter replied in no uncertain terms through Stanton. He ascribed the collapse in the currency and the great destitution to the "treason, insurrection and rebellion against the authority, Constitution and laws of the United States incited and carried on for the last four years by Mr. Brown and his confederate rebels and traitors." He went on to assert that the trouble they were now in was a just penalty for the crimes of treason and rebellion, that the restoration of peace and order could not be entrusted to rebels and traitors, and that the Georgia legislature would not be allowed to usurp legislative powers that might be employed to further fresh acts of treason and

62 *Official Records*, Series I, Vol. XLVII, pt. 2, pp. 107, 114. Sherman, II, p. 253. There is evidence to suggest that some Georgians urged Sherman to give South Carolina some of the same medicine that had been administered to Georgia, and more if possible. See, e.g., New York *World*, January 31, 1865; *Official Records*, Series I, Vol. XLIV, p. 743.

63 Townsend Collection, Vol. 53, no. 263.

64 Townsend Collection, Vol. 54, no. 279; report of Samuel W. Mason, correspondent of the New York *Herald*, March 13, 1865.

65 Savannah *Republican*, January 28, 1865.

66 Bonner, p. 322.

67 General Robert Toombs of Georgia and many other prominent Confederates fled the country; Toombs escaped through the back door of his house in Washington, Wilkes county, as Federal soldiers came through the gates. For an excellent account of what happened to Georgia's Confederate leaders after the war see W. B. Hesseltine and L. Gara, "Georgia's Confederate Leaders after Appomattox," *Georgia Historical Quarterly*, Vol. XXV (1951), p. 1. See also Cobb Collection, Kate Thompson to Mrs. Cobb, September 17, 1865, a gossipy and somewhat malicious account of people like Breckenridge, Benjamin, and the Slidells enjoying life in Paris. For an interesting account of Breckenridge's escape see the Wharncliffe Papers, September 6, 1865 (Sheffield Public Library).

68 U. B. Phillips, ed., *Correspondence of Robert Toombs, Alexander H. Stephens and Howell Cobb*, Annual Report of American Historical Association (Washington, 1915), Vol. II, p. 662.

69 *Official Records*, Series I, Vol. XLIX, pt. 2, pp. 628–630. Allen D. Candler, ed., *The Confederate Records of the State of Georgia* (Atlanta, 1909), Vol. III, pp. 717, 718.

rebellion.[70] General Q. A. Gillmore, commanding the Department of
the South, trusted neither the loyalty of Brown nor that of the leading
politicians of the state; he ordered General Washburn to move a brigade of infantry from Augusta to Milledgeville to prevent the legislature's assembling and to arrest those who arrived.[71] Meanwhile orders
had gone from Stanton to Wilson for Brown's arrest and for him to
be sent incommunicado to Washington; this was done at Milledgeville
on May 9.[72] Brown was sent to Washington but confined for only
about a week and then released on parole.[73]

The end of Brown's governorship left the state in a position of sus-
pended political animation and gave Georgians the opportunity to
take stock of what the war had cost. The physical devastation of
Georgia was substantial, but it later was inflated out of proportion
to actuality by contemporaries and Southern historians who were
racked by the passions engendered by reconstruction. The damage
done from Atlanta to Savannah extended over an area little more than
a fortieth of the state's acreage, albeit some of its richest areas, and
the major part of Georgia remained untouched by actual warfare.
Georgia could not allow other states to wear brighter haloes of mar-
tyrdom than hers, and so "the march to the sea" was created as a
symbol of the sufferings of the South. The real cost of the war would
be paid for in the coinage of political, social, economic, and psycho-
logical readjustment consequent upon the emancipation of the Negro.

---

70   *Official Records,* Series I, Vol. XLIX, pt. 2, pp. 646–647. Candler, ed., III,
p. 719. Johnson did, however, offer clemency to all private persons and "good
people" who should return to their allegiance.
71   *Official Records,* Series I, Vol. XLVII, pt. 3, p. 464.
72   *Ibid.,* Series I, Vol. XLVII, pt. 3, p. 505; Vol. XLIX, pt. 2, p. 702; Candler,
ed., III, p. 721. Alexander H. Stephens and Benjamin H. Hill were arrested at about
the same time.
73   Candler, ed., III, p. 729. Miss Thompson (p. 145) suggests that Brown continued to exercise considerable influence over Andrew Johnson after his release and
telegrams from the Johnson MSS go far to substantiate this suggestion. Indeed, the
indications are that Brown had already realized the necessity for close cooperation
with the federal government over the reconstruction of the state.

II

THE AFTERMATH
OF WAR

More words, more pages, more books have been written about the South than, probably, any other part of the United States because of the uniqueness and the pathos of this great social laboratory. The fascination with the southern states which had mounted steadily before the Civil War continued undiminished with the end of hostilities. Government observers, newspaper correspondents, and interested travelers descended upon the Confederate states and reported at length on the war's damage and distress, on the views of Southerners of all sections of society regarding the measures necessary to rebuild the South and to reincorporate it in the nation, on the region's potential for economic development, and on the situation of the newly-enfranchised Negro. Georgia received her share of attention from observers both sympathetic and antipathetic to her as they raked and rummaged through the ruins of her economy. In detail, reports were often contradictory and confusing, depending upon which parts of the state were being visited and at what time, but in general they provide a clear, broad picture.

The price Georgia paid for her participation in the war cannot be measured in dollars and cents with anything but rough inexactitude. In 1860 Georgia had a population of some 462,000 slaves,[1] which can

---

1   *U.S. Census, 1860*, p. 72, Table no. 2.

be valued at anything between $450 and $500 million. Emancipation rendered this investment a total loss, though many slaveowners hoped that some compensation might be forthcoming from the federal government. The state debt stood at some $20 million, of which $18 million were subsequently repudiated as an essential prerequisite for re-entry to the Union. Banks, insurance companies, and finance houses were almost all in a state of total collapse and Confederate currency in the hands of individuals for all that it was worth could have been used as wallpaper. The New York *World* did indeed report that a member of General Grover's staff was taking Confederate bonds and currency to Savannah sufficient "to start a small paper mill." [2] The confiscation and subsequent taxation of cotton imposed by the federal government, together with the largely abortive attempt to collect Georgia's share of the tax levied in 1861 for the subjugation of the South, only increased the state's financial difficulties and retarded recovery. [3]

The physical destruction carried out mainly between Atlanta and Savannah was plain enough to every observer, but even in those parts of the state where the armies had not penetrated there was evidence of the strain that had been placed upon the state's resources by the necessity of having to live for so long off its own fat. The land bore testimony to neglect; livestock had disappeared, fencing had been broken down or burned, houses and outbuildings left unrepaired, clothing patched and darned, and food had to be secured on a system of barter rather than by cash. One landowner near Savannah maintained that his plantation in July 1865 was so completely wrecked that it would be cheaper and easier "to go into the wild wilderness and clear the forest than attempt the reclamation of my lands." [4]

In this lean period after the war there was considerable distress, much of it very real, some of it imagined, much of it among the colored people, some of it among the whites. At the end of May, Brigadier-General E. F. Winslow reported the desperate situation of many in the counties around Atlanta. He estimated that in ten counties there were some five thousand to eight thousand families comprising twenty-five thousand to fifty thousand persons who were utterly destitute, without bread or any other kind of food. He maintained that some women and children were trudging anything up to forty miles to get food and even then were only able to secure a fraction of their needs. Winslow was fully aware that the state government should in fact be responsible for the relief of its citizens, but as there *was* no state government there was no alternative but that the federal government should assume this responsibility if considerable suffering were to be avoided.[5] Corn and other supplies in Atlanta were distributed through the inferior courts of the various surrounding counties, but Winslow considered that the system had many defects and that frequently injustice was done to many who were genuinely in need.[6] Stores on hand soon proved to be inadequate and the only sure way of securing sufficient supplies was by way of the Western and Atlantic Railroad. A large force was set to work repairing the line between Atlanta and Dalton in north Georgia, though for a while the work was held up by a shortage of tools.[7]

On June 14 Winslow was able to report that in one week alone ending June 10 about forty-five thousand pounds of meat, the same amount of cornmeal, and ten thousand pounds of flour had been distributed. Although he had been warned not to let distribution get out of hand, so great was the demand on supplies that when distributing to the limit he was still only able to relieve a quarter of those in need and then only for about seven days.[8] By June 21 a firm estimate had been made that it would require eight hundred bushels of corn and thirty thousand pounds of meat daily to feed the starving poor of that section of the state adjacent to Atlanta.[9] Some further relief was secured by the dispatch of fifty thousand rations from Apalachicola in Florida,[10] but of necessity the army's ad hoc measures for tackling the problem of destitution in this part of the state were not adequate. In Atlanta itself it was estimated that about fifteen thousand people were helped in the month of June by the distribution of ninety-five

---

2 May 25, 1865.
3 Bonner, pp. 317–318.
4 R. N. Gourdin Papers, Edward C. Anderson letter, July 24, 1865. See also Robert Battey Collection, Battey to his sister, July 19, 1865.
5 *Official Records*, Series I, Vol. XLIX, pt. 2, p. 939.
6 *Ibid.*, p. 945. General Wilson on June 4 instructed him to arrest and remove any civil agent who discriminated between Unionists and rebels when distributing supplies. *Ibid.*, p. 956.
7 *Ibid.*, p. 949.
8 *Ibid.*, p. 992.
9 *Ibid.*, p. 1020.
10 *Ibid.*

thousand pounds of breadstuffs, the same amount of meat, together with salt, coffee, sugar, soap, and candles. About ten clerks assisted by twenty Negro helpers were employed in this task and were kept on the go from morning to night and sometimes far into the night as well. The problem of feeding the civilian population of both races was made more difficult by the increasing numbers of Confederate soldiers discharged from Northern prisoner-of-war camps who had also to be furnished with rations.

Distress was thus widespread, but the speed with which the city of Atlanta began to rebuild indicates that part of this was temporary and occasioned to a considerable extent by the movement of former slaves from the plantations to the city, where freedom was more assured but employment sometimes more elusive. Within six months Atlanta saw the beginnings of a new city, a fact commented on by nearly all observers.

Sidney Andrews, one of the most perceptive of these, noticed that the streets were alive from morning to night with carts, barrows, and wagonloads of timber, brick, and sand. Skilled workmen like carpenters and masons were in great demand and he estimated that four thousand were hard at work rebuilding the city with employment available for another five thousand.[11] The railroads centering on Atlanta were doing a great trade in freight and passenger traffic, the line to Chattanooga alone clearing $100,000 a month, though somewhat restricted in its operations by a shortage of engines and rolling stock.[12] Whitelaw Reid, who traveled through the South from May 1865 to May 1866, came to much the same conclusion as he saw stores reopening at a great rate despite a shortage of building material and the fast-rising price of land. This frontier boomtown aspect of Atlanta's rebirth was marked by much lawlessness; Reid found the streets dangerous after dark.[13] Sir John Kennaway, too, during his stay there, remarked upon the lawlessness of Atlanta and maintained that life and property were insecure and outrages of frequent occurrence despite the streets' being patrolled by the military at night. The Englishman's views may have been a little jaundiced: his initial introduction to Atlanta was not of the best; he had to plod through deep, sticky mud after dark with the aid of a Negro carrying a lantern, all the way from the railroad station to his hotel, where he found "beefsteaks of the consistency of leather, pork fixings (broiled), molasses, cornbread and rye-coffee."[14] He found frame houses going up in all parts of the city and more substantial buildings on the main streets where frontage was fetching $40 a foot.[15] The darker side of the picture was that in a camp about a mile from the city a thousand freedmen were living in wretched conditions on surplus rations provided by the government, and on the other side of the city eight hundred white families were living in similar squalor.[16] This aspect of life in Atlanta was also commented on by J. T. Trowbridge, the well-known Boston writer, who likened the wretched hovels, with their roofs of jagged pieces of tin sheeting held down by rocks to "a fantastic encampment of gypsies or Indians." [17] Most of the business blocks he found to be one-story structures with cheap temporary roofs. Rents were high; $15–$20 a month was being asked for huts which "a respectable farmer would hardly consider good enough for his swine." [18]

In August, Carl Schurz, who had been sent on a fact-finding mission to the South by President Andrew Johnson, was informed that bands of guerillas were active in the surrounding countryside which made it dangerous for individuals and particularly freedmen to venture too far from the city. Some Negroes came into Atlanta while he was there with bullet and buckshot wounds, suffered, they maintained, when they tried to leave plantations in the interior.[19] Christmas 1865 in Atlanta was hardly one of comfort and joy. A correspondent of the *Nation*, arriving on Christmas Eve, found it completely cheerless, ankle-deep in mud, scaffolding, bricks, mortar, and sand left lying around unfinished houses, and with groups of rough-looking men lounging around the liquor shanties.[20] Sticky red mud seemed inevitably to be associated with Atlanta and in places the only way to cross the street was on steppingstones rising out of the ooze. People lived where best they could in wooden shanties or in old army tents and on every hand

---

11   Andrews, pp. 338–340.
12   *Ibid.*, p. 341.
13   Whitelaw Reid, *After the War* (New York, 1866), p. 355.
14   Sir John Kennaway, *On Sherman's Track* (London, 1867), pp. 107, 109.
15   *Ibid.*, pp. 115–116.
16   *Ibid.*, p. 110.
17   *The Desolate South, 1865–1866* (Hartford, 1866), p. 453.
18   *Ibid.*, p. 454.
19   Carl Schurz, *Report on Conditions in the South*, Senate Ex. Doc. no. 2, 39 Cong., 1 sess., Vol. I, p. 18.
20   January 25, 1866.

there were beggars who lived on the emetic pokeweed and pepper-grass boiled in water without salt.[21] A report of one unusual enter-prise was somewhat gruesome: a shrewd gentleman had set to work to collect the bones of dead animals which he then shipped to points on the Athens branch road where they were ground down into fer-tilizer; the report had it that "Among the piles of bones collected for shipment there were some that presented a different appearance from those of four-legged animals." [22]

Outside of Atlanta, recovery was not always as feverish and the period of disillusionment and apathy was more sustained. For in-stance, a brigade of Federal cavalry reached Athens in May and did a certain amount of pillaging of private residences and their smoke-houses. The town suffered very little war damage but the streets re-mained unlighted, washed into gullies or overgrown with grass. Broken windows were covered with paper and fences were propped up with stakes. Business, apart from a desultory country trade, was at a stand-still. A little cloth and thread was being produced with worn-out ma-chinery, and the mills were grinding only sufficient corn and wheat to feed the townspeople.[23] Athens thus provided a good example of the indirect effects of a war of attrition.

One of the most graphic descriptions of affairs in Georgia in the immediate postwar period is that of Eliza Frances Andrews, who lived in the town of Washington, Georgia. Her father, Judge Garnett An-drews, was a staunch Unionist but his family and particularly Eliza revealed the deep bitterness felt by the women of the South at the defeat of the Confederacy. In May 1865 she wrote in her journal that "it did seem a pity to break up a great nation about a parcel of African savages . . . Since the Yankees have treated us so abominably, burn-ing and plundering our country and bringing a gang of Negro soldiers here to insult us, I don't see how anybody can tolerate the sight of their odious old flag again." [24]

In Washington, she said, the streets were so full of idle Negroes and Federal soldiers that ladies scarcely ventured to go out-of-doors, and the country around Clarksville was infested with bushwhackers and robbers. Some of these, she asserted, were poor people who had taken to bushwhacking as the only way to keep themselves alive.[25] In Augusta she heard that Negroes were plaguing the Federal officers for food which was not to be had and the planters were refusing to take these Negroes back once they had left their plantations.[26] Not unnaturally for a girl of her upbringing, she was deeply shocked to see Northern troops publicly dancing with Negro women and walking about the streets with them on their arms.[27] By August, Washington was crowded with freedmen who lived together in parts of the town where white people avoided going if at all possible. There was little work for the Negroes to do in the town, and she concluded that the only way they were able to keep alive was by what they could steal.[28]

Similar feelings were expressed at Augusta in east Georgia, where the stationing of Negro troops seemed to be the main burden of complaint. It was considered that their presence there was a blatant encouragement to the free Negroes to indulge in outrage, murder, and robbery. Constant depradations were being made on fields, gardens, and houses, and it was found difficult, if not impossible, to establish the identity of the thieves.[29] The attitude in Augusta would seem to have been when in doubt, blame the freed Negroes. Like many towns in Georgia, Augusta had been virtually untouched by the war and most of her handsome houses remained intact. Her steamboats on the Savannah river were broken down — as one observer put it "mere rafts propelled by steam." The *Amazon,* a side-wheeler, looked exactly like a roofed barge without either cabins or officers' quarters, and the *Jeff Davis* did not even have a roof.[30] A considerable amount of cotton — one estimate was fifty thousand bales — had been stored in and about Augusta,[31] and some heavy sheetings were being made and sold at twenty-two cents a yard.[32]

By June, peaches, melons, and apples were coming onto the market

---

21 Kate Massey, "A Picture of Atlanta in the Late Sixties," *Atlanta Historical Bulletin,* V (1940), p. 32.

22 New Orleans *Picayune,* December 6, 1865.

23 A. L. Hull, *Annals of Athens, Georgia, 1801–1901* (Athens, 1906), pp. 295, 299–300.

24 Spencer B. King, Jr., ed., *The War-time Journal of a Georgia Girl, 1864–1865, Eliza Frances Andrews* (Macon, 1960), p. 220.

25 *Ibid.,* pp. 253–255.

26 *Ibid.*

27 *Ibid.,* p. 267.

28 *Ibid.,* p. 365.

29 New York *World,* July 11, 1865.

30 *Ibid.*

31 Andrews, p. 353. Kennaway, p. 123n, put the amount of cotton much higher, at 80,000 bales.

32 New York *World,* July 11, 1865.

and provided some variety of diet from the hog and hominy which were the mainstay of most people.[33] By the end of the year the prospects were much brighter. A correspondent of the *Nation* commented favorably on Augusta as a well-built town with broad, level streets bustling with people and vehicles. Warehouses and shops carried a wide range of goods; capital from the North was being invested in the older commercial houses while efforts were being made to interest Northerners in leasing plantations at low prices.[34] Life in Augusta, although not approaching the standards enjoyed before the war, was nothing like as harsh as in some parts of the state.

At Columbus, for example, there was a great deal of actual suffering, particularly among the widows and orphans of Confederate soldiers; [35] even formerly well-to-do families were having to subsist on a diet of cornbread, bacon, and buttermilk, plus an occasional chicken.[36] The correspondent of the *World* painted a drab and depressing picture indeed of Columbus,

in this out-of-the-way town, where not a distinguishing note marks it in the popular eye, Sunday is observed with great punctiliousness especially by the blacks: but all other days pass by in stupid, idle vacancy. This place has been so long and so completely shut out from the light of life that the advent of a stranger is an episode. Outside of Macon and Columbus there are no towns in S.W. Georgia of note and the lower counties are almost a primeval wilderness. . . .

He maintained further that poverty was so prevalent that many women were boarding the trains without money and trusting to the good nature of the conductors not to be put off again.[37]

By September, the New Orleans *Picayune* was able to report that flatboats were being built at Columbus to transport cotton on the Chattahoochee river to Apalachicola, which rather belied the picture of stagnation presented by the *World*.[38]

In contradistinction, business in Macon revived relatively quickly. This town of some eight thousand people, with broad, pleasant streets, lay at the head of steamboat navigation on the Ocmulgee river and at the center of Georgia's railroad network; it was one of the most important of the interior towns of the state and had been a major point of refuge during the closing stages of the war. Refugees continued to crowd into it, and in the interests of good order, General Wilson endeavored to restrict the surplus population of both white refugees and plantation Negroes.[39] Once the railroads were rebuilt and in full operation again, the future of Macon was assured, although never likely to approach the phenomenal development of Atlanta.

The recovery of Savannah exhibited little of the energy that characterized Atlanta and the British consul there, W. Tasker-Smith, wrote home to the Foreign Office somewhat ponderously in June 1865, "with crippled capital and impoverished resources, it has not been possible, hitherto, for any extension of trade to take place: but there are signs that the body Commercial in this state still possesses vitality and though the pulsations are feeble and irregular, they indicate returning powers." He estimated that there were about three hundred thousand bales of cotton still scattered about the state, but the major difficulty was transportation. A few small river steamers were bringing some downriver from Augusta, but he saw little prospect of British ships' securing return cargoes for three to six months.[40] The impressions of a correspondent of the New York *World*, writing on the same day from Savannah, were completely different. He reported that there were seagoing ships tied up at the wharves with tenders white with cotton alongside. He was pleased to find that Northern newspapers, novels, and periodicals were on sale in the streets, though he was somewhat put out at his inability to find a good hotel.[41] Whether Tasker-Smith was deliberately preparing his defense beforehand should British shipowners complain to the British government that they could not secure cargoes, or whether the *World*'s correspondent was concerned to such an extent with the problem of good hotel accommodation that he gave no more than a superficial glance at the commercial situation of the city is a matter of opinion, but there can be little doubt of the partisan

---

33   *Ibid.*

34   *Nation*, January 25, 1866.

35   Alexander H. Stephens Papers, M. I. Crawford to A.H.S., October 6, 1865. Crawford's plantations had suffered considerably at the hands of General Wilson's troops.

36   New York *World*, July 18, 1865.

37   *Ibid.*

38   New Orleans *Picayune*, September 12, 1865.

39   *Ibid.*, June 23, 1865. Wilson was very well thought of in Macon, and Howell Cobb considered him both courteous and gentlemanly. Phillips, ed., p. 663.

40   Public Record Office, London, F.O.5, *America II Series*, Savannah, June 28, 1865.

41   New York *World*, July 11, 1865.

clarity of the feelings of one Southern woman writing from the city in late July:

My heart is filled with an intensity of hatred toward the authors of our misery that I cannot mollify . . . If we go to our street doors to catch a breath of fresh air we are annoyed by the sight of armed Yankees (white and black). I cannot reconcile myself to this wretched state of servitude. How can Southerners for a moment forget the wrongs they have suffered. Yet many associate with Yankees and say "Let byegones be byegones." Our market is bountifully supplied and prices comparatively moderate. . . . The city is comparatively healthy — Negroes and Yankees furnish food for disease. The police regulations are admirable — Savannah has never been so scrupulously clean. Robberies are frequent and daring — they are generally traced to Negroes who are invariably punished severely. They begin to realize that freedom is not bliss. Poor deluded creatures! [42]

By October the business prospects of the city were taking an upturn and many Northerners were in Savannah investigating the prospects for investment of capital in new enterprises. The wharves were becoming increasingly busy and the lumber trade looked particularly promising.[43] Refugees both black and white continued to flock into the city and Andrews reports some two thousand respectable persons in and around Savannah as dependent on charity, whilst hundreds of Negroes were dying of starvation, having been turned off or left plantations to the north and west with little or no money and only a few bushels of corn.[44]

All the major towns and cities of Georgia were affected differently by the destruction of industry and railroad facilities and the number of refugees they were required to absorb. But they did have something in common: the problem of the newly-freed Negroes who sought both the guarantee of their freedom there under the closer protection of the Federal forces and the relief they needed from the same source. To a degree, the cities and towns found themselves in a position not unlike that of the larger plantations before the war with the Negroes living in separate quarters, dependent largely upon the whites for sustenance and employment, although the compulsive authority of the former slaveowners was lacking to make the Negro work in order to live. The skills of the majority of Negroes were unsuitable for employment in the towns and cities at a time when these same cities, under adverse circumstances, were endeavoring to recover from the effects of the war. Ironically, the highly-skilled Negro craftsman who as a slave had been prominent in the life of many towns, now as a freedman, however much his skills could have been utilized, was not allowed to compete with white workers. The demand for his labor was not sufficient to overcome the fear and resentment of his competition.[45]

In contrast, the immediate problems of the rural areas of Georgia were those of a somewhat different kind. Where the cities were suffering an embarrassment of unwanted riches in former slaves, the rural areas were faced with the problem of a labor force decreased and decreasing as the result of migration to the towns and to other states, and the large-scale withdrawal of female labor from work in the fields. Moreover, control of the labor force that remained by the simple right of ownership was now lacking. The violent transition from slavery to freedom necessitated radical readjustment and revolutionary new ideas to deal with what would have to be a complete recasting of agricultural methods; it is not surprising that in many rural areas the slave system was only reluctantly given up and attitudes fostered over two centuries only agonizingly changed. Many people in the rural areas had had their plantations and farms physically devastated by the armies, both Union and Confederate, that had marched across them, but emancipation, although some were slow to realize its implications, destroyed much more. The benevolent paternalism which had come so easily to most slaveowners was replaced too often by race hatred of the most virulent kind.[46]

Recovery in the rural areas of Georgia was hampered by the drought which set in within a month or two of the end of the war. One summing up of the situation before the full effects of the drought had been felt was given by the overseer on Howell Cobb's Hurricane plantation in Baldwin county in July; "Some of the crop looks very well while other

---

42   Barnsley Collection, Rebecca Mimms to Mrs. Barnsley, July 27, 1865.
43   R. N. Gourdin Papers, Anderson to Gourdin, October 18, 1865.
44   Andrews, pp. 365–369. See also Reid, p. 150.
45   S. D. Spero and A. L. Harris, *The Black Worker* (Columbia University Press, 1931), p. 15.
46   The long-accepted view is that the main source of anti-Negro feeling came from "poor whites" being thrown into economic competition with the Negro and determined to maintain superiority based on the color of the skin alone. This is in keeping with the myth that such attitudes were below the dignity of well-born and highminded Southern gentlemen, but expressions of hatred for the Negro can be found among all classes of society.

potion of it will not make ennything . . . the negrows have kild nearly all the hoggs that is of enny size . . . We air out of corn and meet — have kild the last beef we have left. Some one stold seven head of cattle from us. Things air in a unfavorable condition on this plantation . . ." [47]

One of the best accounts of the difficulties of those in the rural areas can be found in a series of letters written by Elisha Lowrey, an overseer of a plantation at Sugar Valley, Gordon county, in northwest Georgia, to his employer, John S. Dobbins. Writing shortly before Christmas 1864, [48] he reported that during the previous spring the Federal forces had taken all the corn and nearly all the meat together with salt, cattle, hogs, and horses. Lowrey was left with little more than the shirt on his back, twenty bushels of wheat, and two milk cows. Nevertheless, with the help of some broken-down horses that had been left behind by the Federal forces, they were able to raise a good crop of corn. The Federal forces then returned and took about seven hundred bushels, leaving him with little more than a hundred. They would probably have taken the lot but "Hood's army come through here and they was so flusterated that they never got here with their waggons." A raiding party ransacked the house, however, and destroyed most of that which had been left after the earlier visit. Fortunately, two hogs which had gone wild turned up again and at a hundred and fifty pounds each provided them with some meat, although they had no salt for preserving. What few stock and fowls that were left were ready to run off at the sight of a bluecoat, and Lowrey bitterly commented, "I never want to see any more blue — I don't care how cheap indigo gets to be." People in the neighborhood were not above denouncing Lowrey to the Union forces and claiming a right to the furniture of the house. Others squatted on the Dobbins's plantation and Lowrey was powerless to prevent them raising a crop off plantation land. Their argument was that it was captured property and therefore as much theirs as Dobbins's.

By the middle of February 1865 [49] Lowrey was nearing the end of what had been left behind by the Federal forces and had no money to buy what corn there was to be had fifteen or twenty miles up the railroad track. Another problem facing him was the Confederate deserters who were stealing for night-riding such horses as still remained. His view was that the Confederate raiders were worse than the Federal soldiers because the latter did at least leave behind broken-down horses in place of fresh ones, whereas the deserters left nothing. He estimated that only one family in five in the neighborhood had enough to live on; between Sugar Valley and Calhoun there was hardly a house intact and many had been torn down completely. Of some significance was the fact, as reported by Lowrey, that many Georgians collaborated with the Federal troops and others moved north taking their slaves with them. He advised Dobbins's plantation Negroes to stay where they were because he had seen "negroes with the Yanks fed on one cracker per day and drove much harder."

One month later [50] Lowrey reported that they were facing starvation, and that heavy rains and flooding were preventing their doing any work. His neighbors who had previously denounced him to the Federal soldiers now denounced him to the Confederate deserters for hoarding provisions. As a result, the rebels burned down his house, and he was daily expecting Dobbins's house to receive the same treatment. No rent was being paid for land in the county and the breakdown of any law enforcement opened the way for land to be taken up for nothing.

By June, as the onset of the drought began to be felt, Lowrey found himself faced with crops in a very sorry condition while personally battling against an attack of scurvy. He estimated that if he could get twenty bushels of corn from fifteen to sixteen acres he would be fortunate. Two acres of beans which he had planted were dead and the peas were in a like state. The people of Gordon and Floyd counties were desperate for corn, and what they received from the Union armies "don't look like it was fit to eat but the people eat it and seem to be thankful that they have it." [51]

At much the same time Howell Cobb was writing to his wife from Sumter county, where he found that the hot, dry summer was cutting in half the expected crop. In addition he was very dubious about the Negro hands he was employing because they did not work as hard as they had when they were slaves. He believed that relying completely on free Negro labor could be extremely dangerous. [52]

---

47   Cobb Collection, J. D. Collins to John A. Cobb, July 9, 1865.
48   J. S. Dobbins Collection, Elisha Lowrey to John S. Dobbins, December 18, 1864.
49   *Ibid.*, February 19, 1865.
50   *Ibid.*, March 19, 1865.
51   *Ibid.*, September 6, 1865.
52   Cobb Collection, Cobb to his wife, September 10, 1865.

A well-balanced account of conditions in the countryside immediately after the war was given by Dr. Robert Battey, who had served with the Confederate forces in Virginia in 1862. Writing to his sister from Rome, Georgia, in July 1865, he maintained that newspaper correspondents, accustomed to easy living, were giving an unnecessarily distorted picture of the hardships being endured by Southerners.

In no instance has it been necessary for me to draw subsistence stores from the Govt. nor have I any idea that such a necessity will arise. Large numbers of our people are drawing from the A.C.S. [Army Commissariat] at Kingston; very many are forced to do so since there is [sic] not provisions enough in the country to subsist the population — but large numbers of those who draw could feed themselves had they manliness to sacrifice their property in place of their honor

The wheat-crop in this section of the country is an entire failure but little land was sown for want of seed and labor . . . I know of but one farmer in this county who has reaped more wheat than will be necessary for his own family consumption . . . the masses must subsist upon corn meal which is likely to be abundant enough for the white population . . . Hundreds of families are subsisting themselves wholly upon cornbread and milk with garden vegetables . . . I have not seen a single stalk of cotton growing in this county — I do not believe that the entire production of the county this year will make 500 pounds — not even 100 pounds. Our farmers have no seed which will vegetate; a striking illustration of the improvidence of our people.[53]

Conditions in the rural areas varied greatly from one county to another and from one part of a county to another. In some parts there was real distress if not actual starvation, in others comparative plenty. To provide a rough equalization and to feed the swelling urban centers, adequate transportation was needed, but this was precisely what Georgia did not have at this time. Before the war the state's transportation system, financed by city and private subscriptions, had been one of the finest in the South; even before the arrival of Northern troops intent upon smashing the South's communications, however, the railroads had been worked far beyond their capacities. The result was that through unavoidable neglect of maintenance and overwork, engines and rolling stock were worn out, then cannibalized. The track itself suffered in much the same fashion, with maintenance and replacement reduced to a minimum. In part, the defeat of the Confederacy can be attributed to the failure of the South's communication system brought on by excessive use, the activities of Sherman and his troops with their

genius for destruction, and, not least, by Sherman's Confederate counterparts who ripped up railroad track rather than allow it to be used
by the Federal forces. Thus the end of the war saw Georgia left with
her railroads in a sorry state. Though technically the 1,420 miles of
railroad in Georgia in 1860 remained in existence in 1865, large
stretches were completely unusable. The chief damage was found on
lines running from Chattanooga via Atlanta and Macon to Savannah.[54]
Sherman in his report to E. M. Stanton on December 13, 1864, estimated that some two hundred miles of track had been destroyed in
the course of his march to Savannah — chiefly the lines of the Macon
and Western and the Central of Georgia.[55] When Trowbridge traveled
through the state in the late summer of 1865 about a hundred miles of
the Central were still not repaired and where it had been possible to
straighten out some of Sherman's "hairpins," "corkscrews," and "neck-
ties" and relay the track, jolting along on hard, wooden seats was far
from comfortable.[56] Traveling in Georgia immediately after the war
was a combination of delay, danger, and discomfort — and at times
very expensive. A correspondent of the *Nation* took six days to travel
from Savannah to Augusta; a speed of fifteen miles an hour was considered fast. Between railheads, where the track was out, parties of three
or four might be charged as much as $25 each for fifty miles by hack.[57]
Sir John Kennaway, when he traveled along the same line, had to cover
the fifty-mile broken stretch in an old military ambulance purchased
from the government.[58] Andrews made the journey from Albany to
Milledgeville at ten miles an hour, the speed being kept down to avoid
accidents resulting from defects in the track.[59] The frequency with
which trains ran off the rails was accepted at this time as a necessary
hazard of traveling. Kennaway, on his journey from Atlanta to Augusta,
found that the railroad carriage he was in was little more than a box
on wheels, the glass broken out of every third or fourth window; it was
crowded with "workmen and darkies" and displayed the ominous notice:

---

53   Robert Battey Collection, July 19, 1865. For a fuller discussion of the agrari-
an problems of Georgia, see below pp. 100ff.
54   *Official Records*, Series III, Vol. V, p. 584.
55   Sherman, II, p. 201.
56   Trowbridge, p. 265.
57   *Nation*, October 5, 1865.
58   Kennaway, p. 155.
59   Andrews, p. 230.

"Passengers are positively forbidden to ride upon the tops or platforms of cars. From the defective condition of the track, the cars are very likely to run off, in which case the danger to passengers is much increased in such a position." [60]

By the end of the year conditions had either improved considerably or Kennaway was unlucky. The correspondent of the *Nation* traveling the same route found the cars comfortable and commodious and traveling at speeds over fourteen miles an hour. The passengers were a mixture of Jews, drummers from New York, and men and a few women from every Southern state. Some slept, others circulated their whiskey flasks. Newspapers from Chicago, Louisville, and Nashville were on sale, and a one-armed Confederate veteran was selling cigars. [61]

Trowbridge found the Western and Atlantic Railroad in poor condition, dilapidated track and temporary bridges replacing those which had been destroyed. It lacked, moreover, machine shops and the materials necessary for the repair of old and worn-out rolling stock. [62]

Both he and Robert Somers reported that the Central of Georgia Railroad had been wise to reserve from its earnings a large fund (Trowbridge placed it at a million and a half dollars) which had been deposited in England and which could now be drawn upon to meet the costs of repairing the road. [63] Contracts were made in 1865 through several New York agents for the supplying of nearly twenty-four hundred tons of English rails and thirty-three hundred tons of American rails which, it was estimated, would be sufficient to relay over ninety miles of track. [64] In March 1866 a more precise figure of 6,694 tons, sufficient for eighty-four miles of track, was given by the president of the road, William M. Wadley. [65] The Central of Georgia was not the only road to get supplies from abroad, and the possibility of purchasing locomotives from Great Britain was considered by the state-owned road. In January 1866 William Schley wrote from Paris to Charles Jenkins, the first duly elected postwar governor of Georgia, suggesting that British locomotives should be bought for the Western and Atlantic Railroad, as credit for ten years could be obtained against an issue of state bonds at seven per cent. In return for gold, he maintained, locomotives could be had for $11,000–$12,000, and wrought iron wheels and cast steel tires and axles for the same price as ordinary cast iron in the United States — "worth three of Northern Manufacture." [66]

The difficulties encountered by the Central of getting back into working order were common to most of the state's railroads. Engines and rolling stock were scattered throughout the South. One locomotive found burned out on the Atlantic and Gulf Railroad had been stripped of all its brass, copper, and flues, and everything that could be carried off had been taken. Another removed to South Carolina by the Confederate authorities had to be left with the South Carolina Railroad Company until such time as the road was opened to Augusta. A number of old engines which had been smashed by order of General Hardee at Savannah remained unusable until new cylinders and other parts could be found. Cars were scattered over five or six states, many burned or otherwise destroyed, some useless until repaired.[67] The final accounting of cars in December 1866 revealed that holdings had dropped from 729 in 1860 to 537 in 1866. Those collected from as far away as Wilmington, North Carolina, were in poor shape; 97 cars had been sold, condemned, or destroyed and 95 had been given up entirely as lost.[68]

By the end of 1865, the road had a deficit of nearly $78,000 on the year's operations, but a hundred and fifty-one miles of track were open. Fifty-eight miles of track were open between Macon and Eatonton, wooden stationhouses were being built and trains were running daily over the thirty-two miles between Augusta and Waynesboro, and daily freight trains on the sixty-one miles between Savannah and Station 6.[69] At the end of the year, however, there was still a thirty-nine-mile gap between Savannah and Augusta and a hundred-and-ten-mile gap between Savannah and Macon; stages had to be used between Savannah and Augusta. It was not until February 1866 that the rails were joined between Savannah and Augusta, and connections were not established with Macon until early in June.[70] Once the junction had been made

60   Kennaway, p. 117.
61   *Nation,* January 25, 1866.
62   Trowbridge, p. 459. This state of affairs swiftly changed, however, under Major Campbell-Wallace.
63   *Ibid.,* p. 502. Robert Somers, *The Southern States since the War* (New York, 1871), p. 72.
64   *Thirtieth Report of the Central Railroad and Banking Company of Georgia,* December 1, 1865, pp. 278–279.
65   *Ibid.,* p. 289.
66   Telamon-Cuyler Collection, Schley to Jenkins, January 31, 1866.
67   *Thirtieth Report of the Central Railroad,* p. 275.
68   *Thirty-first Report of the Central Railroad,* p. 388.
69   *Thirtieth Report of the Central Railroad,* pp. 275–276.
70   *Ibid.,* p. 294.

between Savannah and Augusta, the company could get access to the bulk of the rolling stock and machinery that had been sent to Augusta for safekeeping at the end of the war.[71] By the end of 1866 over a million dollars had been spent by the company on reconstructing the road, but the accounts also showed that between April 1865 and December 1866 there was a surplus of nearly three quarters of a million dollars from earnings, once ordinary expenses had been deducted.[72] More hands had to be employed on the road as less work seemed to be done than under the slave system (an estimated fourteen per cent production drop each month). The morale of the labor force was high, though, because the men were paid promptly. On the other hand, they were discharged without ceremony for disobedience.[73]

Though the Western and Atlantic Railroad had also taken a heavy beating, it showed considerable powers of recuperation. For more than a year after September 1864, this road was operated by the federal military authorities and as a temporary measure those portions of the track which had not been completely destroyed were relaid with burned rails on inferior cross ties of pine or poplar.[74] One estimate is that at the end of the war little more than eight passenger and baggage cars and three hundred and fifty-one freight cars were of any use.[75] Many of the cars and engines had been used beyond the limits of safety and were scattered in Virginia, South Carolina, and different parts of Georgia. To get the road going again required quite substantial replacements. The state therefore bought from the federal government eight locomotives, a hundred and forty box cars, and forty-five passenger cars and three stationary engines for pumping water and running car shop machinery. The rebuilding of bridges was initially held up for want of lumber, and for a while guards had to be employed along some stretches of the road to protect property and merchandise from the thieves who infested the road.[76] Nevertheless, despite considerable difficulties, the superintendent of the road was able to report in December 1865 that from September 25 to November 1, 1865, the line had a net income of $120,718 on gross earnings of $170,793, although payment to the East Tennessee and Georgia Railroad Company for the use of track from the junction near Chickamauga station to Chattanooga had not as yet been made.[77] The sum total of purchases made from the United States government was $464,152, and bonds were needed pledging the faith of the state to pay off the debt within two years at an interest rate of seven and three tenths per cent per annum.[78] The state-owned road was in a particularly favorable situation for securing credit, but in subsequent years applications for state aid to other railroads were pressed hard, granted, and came to provide a rare opportunity for malfeasance at all levels.[79]

Thus the postwar scene in Georgia was not of the brightest. The plantations which had contributed greatly to her prosperity before the war were rundown and neglected, livestock had been butchered or run off, and the labor force of slaves had been emancipated but also left footloose and sometimes irresponsible. Her industries, such as they were, and her railroad network had been overworked or wrecked by the Northern armies. The people who had survived four years of war had little to show for their efforts on behalf of the Confederacy but handfuls of valueless paper which was useless for filling empty bellies. Destitution and hunger were kissing cousins of defeat — Georgia was exhausted and clubbed to her knees. It was not the best of times nor the worst of times. An army of occupation was galling to Southern pride, but it also provided money, food, and clothing. Moreover, its presence was an assurance to those who feared that their former slaves might take vengeance on them that they were safe, if occasionally hungry. The cost of the war was a savage one, but recovery was suprisingly swift. Military rule was, for the most part, efficient but temporary and only two major problems needed solution: firstly, when and with what sort of government would Georgia be readmitted to the Union; secondly, how soon and how far would the former slaves be admitted into citizenship and how drastic would the change in their status be upon the economic and social life of Georgia. Fundamentally, Georgia's future would hinge upon the solutions to these interacting problems.

---

71 *Thirty-first Report of the Central Railroad,* p. 314.
72 *Ibid.,* p. 304.
73 *Ibid.,* p. 326.
74 James H. Johnston, *The Western and Atlantic Railroad of the State of Georgia . . .* (Atlanta, 1932), p. 58.
75 *Ibid.,* p. 59.
76 Candler, ed., IV, pp. 122ff.
77 *Ibid.*
78 *Ibid.,* p. 480.
79 See below, p. 202. Roads like the Macon and Western between Atlanta and Macon and the Georgia Railroad suffered comparatively little damage and the latter in particular prospered for a while from the lack of competition from other roads. Thompson, pp. 106–107.

III

POLITICAL
RECONSTRUCTION
The First Phase

GEORGIA was ruled under a scorching travesty of law, alternating with bayonet despotism governed by mob caprice; this era of whimsical yet savage tyranny, known by the abhorrent name of RECONSTRUCTION, must ever remain the ridicule of patriotism and the contempt of statesmanship. It was the spawn of unbridled might. It violated every principle of good government. It sported wantonly with the sacred axiom of civil liberty. Inspired by hate and operated with malice, it abortively retarded for a decade of years the very object it claimed to seek, viz: — a solid and fraternal rehabilitation of a sundered Union and warring people.[1]

This classical definition of Reconstruction in Georgia by an editor of the Atlanta *Constitution* who was personally involved in the events about which he was writing would have been accepted without question as a correct interpretation of the decade after the Civil War by most Southern historians until about 1940, when "revisionist" historians like Howard K. Beale, Francis B. Simkins, and A. A. Taylor began their Sisyphean labors of trying to examine the period dispassionately and judiciously.[2] Avery, who in passages like the above was doing little more than stoking the furnaces of his own hysteria, would possibly still be considered a sound interpreter of Reconstruction by some historians like E. M. Coulter, but his views would doubtless have caused considerable perplexity to those Federal officers who were faced with the manifold problems of what to do with the Southern states once they had been subdued. Lincoln's plans for the readmission of the Southern states to the Union, based on compassion and an admonitory rapping of knuckles, would have stood little chance of acceptance in the face of the realities of the postwar situation. Andrew Johnson, his successor, lacking Lincoln's political finesse, had even less chance of securing their acceptance however much he might modify them. The struggle which would develop in Washington over the reconstruction of the South was of little help to those on the spot who had to cope with the multifarious problems occasioned by the defeat of the Confederacy. They could only work from day to day, doing their best to interpret what was in the minds of those in Washington who sent directives not always of crystal clarity. Avery's "bayonet despotism" and "savage tyranny" would have evoked only puzzlement from commanders whose forces were rapidly diminishing from overswift demobilization and who were only too willing to transfer their unwanted problems to some responsible civil government. Observers like Schurz, Major-General Steedman, and Brigadier-General John T. Croxton complained steadily that they could see little loyalty to the Union among the people of Georgia.[3] This naivety and lack of comprehension which considered that the loyalty which had sustained so many through four years of war could be thrown away like an old shirt was only paralleled by a like naivety on the part of some Georgians who hoped that the federal government would be quite happy to permit the reinstitution of state government by prominent secessionists and leaders of the defunct Confederacy. At the same time the very outrageousness of the assumption that they could be allowed to re-establish government in

---

1 I. W. Avery, *History of the State of Georgia from 1850 to 1881* (New York, 1881), p. 335.

2 Howard K. Beale, "On Rewriting Reconstruction History," *American Historical Review,* XLV (1940), pp. 807–827; Francis B. Simkins, "New Viewpoints of Southern Reconstruction," *Journal of Southern History,* V (1939), pp. 49–61; A. A. Taylor, "Historians of Reconstruction," *Journal of Negro History,* XXIII (1938), pp. 16–34. The great Negro apologist, W. E. B. DuBois, had much earlier in "Reconstruction and Its Benefits," *American Historical Review,* XV (1910), pp. 781–799, begun in Marxist fashion to examine the dark underbelly of Reconstruction, but in this article and in his *Black Reconstruction* (1935) he redressed the balance so violently in his righteous indignation that all his colored geese became snow-white swans.

3 Schurz, Senate Ex. Doc. no. 2, 39 Cong., 1 sess., Vol. I, 6 and 7, pp. 52–53.

this form would suggest that able politicians such as Governor Joseph E. Brown, who could never be accused of being unrealistic, were anxious to see how much could be secured by calculated effrontery.[4]

Before Brown was arrested and had to surrender the governorship, he was, however, able to authorize Leopold Waitzfelder of Milledgeville to go to Britain as the state's agent and secure from Charles H. Reid and Company of London all money held on account by them and owing to Georgia for cotton sold. Waitzfelder was also authorized to see Henry Lafone of Liverpool for the same purpose, and, further, to go to Nassau and have shipped to Europe or wherever he could get a good price, all blankets, shoes, cloth, soldier's clothing, and equipment and all other property of the state stored in Nassau, Bermuda, and other places abroad.[5]

With Brown no longer available as governor, the question arose regarding the best man to put forward as provisional governor. General Alfred H. Colquitt, a large plantation owner, future industrialist, and after 1872 with John B. Gordon and Brown a member of the "Bourbon triumvirate," was suggested as suitable for the position. Another name considered was that of Henry L. Benning, a prominent prewar secessionist and distinguished soldier, although his somewhat profane language made him unacceptable to many religious people.[6] Joshua Hill strongly urged his own qualifications as a staunch Unionist upon Andrew Johnson but the final choice for provisional governor fell upon James Johnson, a lawyer from Columbus, who was a good choice in that he had had some experience in Congress, had been opposed to secession in 1861, and had taken no active part in the conflict. Less violently Unionist than Joshua Hill, he was more "available" and not likely to antagonize important political elements at a very critical juncture.[7] On June 17, 1865, he was proclaimed provisional governor at a salary of $3,000 a year and was instructed by President Andrew Johnson to call together a convention composed of loyal Georgians who could take the Amnesty Oath of May 29, 1865, for the purpose of amending the Constitution of Georgia. Over-all authority remained with the military, but the provisional governor had the power to appoint civil officials whose loyalty could be assured.[8] At the same time the attorney-general in Washington warned him against indiscriminate pardoning under the Amnesty Proclamation and in each case demanded information whether proceedings had been instituted against the petitioner under the confiscation acts and whether any of the petitioner's property was held by the United States government as "abandoned property."[9]

Governor Johnson quickly dispelled the illusions of some Georgians who were still hoping that some modified form of slavery could be retained. At Macon he made it quite clear publicly that he considered the war to have been a piece of stupendous folly of their own making. To a loyal meeting in Savannah he stated, "Slavery . . . is gone and gone forever and I have no tears to shed or lamentations to make over its departure."[10] On July 13 he issued a proclamation calling for an election of delegates to a convention on the first Wednesday of October 1865. The delegates to the convention were to assemble at Milledgeville on the fourth Wednesday of that same month. Both electors and delegates were required to have subscribed to the Amnesty Oath, and as there was no civil law in operation, the military would be responsible for dealing with any breaches of the peace. For good measure,

---

4 Governor Brown, although not occupying the center of the political stage after his forced resignation in 1865, was a key figure throughout the Reconstruction period and the oft-repeated quip that Avery, a firm supporter of Brown, should have entitled his book "The History of Joe Brown's Georgia" has more than a modicum of truth to it. Brown's election as the Democratic candidate for governor in 1857 by a large majority over Benjamin H. Hill, the Know-Nothing candidate, came as a shock to the old aristocratic regime in Georgia. This virtually unknown farmer (in 1857) from the North Georgia mountains was a worthy representative of the yeoman farmers (the "wool hats," according to his opponents). He had raised himself as a lawyer and politician by his own abilities and aggressive leadership to the highest offices in the state. His election, in effect, was a revolution in political leadership predating that usually attributed to the results of the Civil War.

5 Telamon-Cuyler Collection, authorization of Waitzfelder by J. E. Brown, May 5, 1865. The extent of Waitzfelder's operations and how far Brown's subsequent rise to affluence in the business world was due to cooperation with him may not be fully known until access can be secured to the Brown papers in the private collection of Mr. Felix Hargrett of New York.

6 Augusta *Constitutionalist*, April 12, 1865, quoted by New York *World*, April 25, 1865. These early suggestions seemingly assumed that Brown could not continue as governor.

7 Andrews, p. 24, described him as "a plain and unassuming gentleman of forty-five to fifty years of age, of medium size and height, who dresses throughout in black, has a regular and pleasantly inexpressive face, wears short chin and throat whiskers and is slightly bald."

8 Candler, ed., IV, p. 8.

9 Telamon-Cuyler Collection, Attorney-General James Speed to Johnson, June 1865.

10 Avery, pp. 341–342n, Savannah *Republican*, July 3, 1865.

he added the warning that any idea that private property would be redistributed was a delusion.[11]

The right to amnesty and the right to participate in the formation of civil government was denied to Confederate military officers above the rank of colonel, to Confederate civil officials, and to citizens whose wealth exceeded $20,000, although individual pardons might be obtained from the president. These provisions, despite the loophole provided of presidential pardon, affected Democratic secessionists most severely, but applied also to many who had at first opposed secession but had gone with the state once secession was a fact and had played a prominent part in the struggle. The result was, as had been expected, that delegates to the convention were drawn from the ranks of those who had been opposed to secession from the beginning and from lukewarm secessionists who had not achieved much prominence.[12] Delegates were predominantly conservative and obscure men who were not given any sort of carte blanche to make drastic amendments to the Constitution of Georgia. While it was recognized that everything pertaining to slavery would have to be erased from the state Constitution, there were early signs that there were those who felt that only free white male citizens should have the franchise, that only free white males should act as jurors, and that the testimony of a freedman should not be accepted in court against that of a white man.[13]

The quality of the men sent to the convention was not necessarily of vital importance. For one correspondent of Howell Cobb the question of representation in Congress, however, was of the utmost concern:

On the subject of our representation in Congress for Heaven's sake let's try and get men who will not misrepresent those of us who have been the true friends of the country . . . a miserable, cringing, cowardly set of men who would urge confiscation and preach of our disloyalty to cover up their own base hypocrisy and treason must be beaten . . . We are only entitled to seven Representatives and we must watch the Districting of the State so as to control the Unionism of the Whig counties. As to the Convention it makes no difference who goes there . . . A good and true body of men in the Legislature is of vast importance.[14]

Opinion seemed to be that of about three hundred delegates who were sent to the convention at Milledgeville, the great majority were conservative mediocrities, men who were politically uncompromised but prepared to seek compromise over the position in which Georgia, like other Southern states, found herself. Andrews mentioned the presence of "seedy politicians" and "rough backwoods fellows."[15] Miss Thompson considered that "the great majority were insignificant men who were not prominent before or after 1865."[16] One biographer of Benjamin H. Hill felt that "it was a reputable body, composed largely of moderate and patriotic individuals who were disposed to accept the new dispensation in good faith."[17] Avery, on the other hand, maintained that "The body was an able one and patriotic and conservative."[18] Woolley, Georgia's first historian of Reconstruction, went even further and termed it "a body distinguished for the reputation and ability of its members."[19] All agreed, however, on the conservative nature of those sent to this Constitutional Convention and although many doubtless bewailed the absence of men of the caliber of Toombs, Cobb, and Stephens, there can be little gainsaying the fact that at this point in Georgia's history more progress was likely to be made by some "rough backwoods fellow" than by someone like the irascible, unrepentant Robert Toombs.

The leadership of the convention fell to two lawyers, both anti-secessionists, Herschel V. Johnson and Charles J. Jenkins. The former became president of the convention, the latter chairman of the committee on business. Herschel V. Johnson, as Andrews saw him, was a man of considerable presence. He was short but heavily built, had long black hair above a receding forehead, and was clean-shaven with cold, steely eyes behind gold-rimmed spectacles. Courteous but aloof, he gave the impression of great strength and vitality.[20] In contrast, Jenkins, over sixty years of age, was a patriarchal figure with snow-white hair and

---

11   Candler, ed., IV, p. 4. In some parts of the more remote mountain areas like Rabun county law enforcement was badly needed. Telamon-Cuyler Collection, Netherland to Johnson, July 22, 1865.

12   Thompson, p. 148.

13   Telamon-Cuyler Collection, W. S. Wallace to Johnson, August 9, 1865.

14   Cobb Collection, Martin J. Crawford to Cobb, September 29, 1865.

15   Andrews, p. 238.

16   Thompson, p. 149.

17   Haywood J. Pearce, Jr., *Benjamin H. Hill, Secession and Reconstruction* (University of Chicago Press, 1928), p. 117.

18   Avery, pp. 347–348.

19   E. C. Woolley, *The Reconstruction of Georgia* (Columbia University Press, 1901), p. 14.

20   Andrews, p. 241.

whiskers.[21] Both men were highly respected and conducted the affairs of the convention with much wisdom.

Johnson, on taking the chair, warned the delegates that the difficulties under which Georgia was laboring required both caution and intelligence if they were to be overcome. Their major task was to rescue the state from the unfortunate consequences of secession.[22] On October 28 the convention received a message from the provisional governor in which he outlined the problems facing the state. The cotton bought by the state had been either captured or burned, and all assets abroad had been drawn upon to the limit. No income was coming in from the state-owned Western and Atlantic Railroad.[23] He described what steps had been taken to replace depots, workshops, ties, rails, and bridges and estimated that $500,000 would be needed to put the line back in full running order. So short of funds was the treasury that he had to borrow $50,000 from the citizens of Augusta to pay the expenses of the delegates to the convention. This shortage of money also meant that the academy for the blind at Macon and the lunatic asylum at Milledgeville were being kept going solely on credit. The penitentiary and its shops were nearly all destroyed, and those convicts who had not been discharged had escaped. The public debt stood at $20,813,525, of which $2,667,750 had been contracted before the war. In Johnson's view, there was no legal or moral obligation to pay the $18,135,775 of this debt which had been incurred in the prosecution of rebellion against the United States. He considered that "the currency and the cause stood and fell together and the currency can be interred in the same grave as the Confederacy." He warned the delegates that any attempt to assume this war debt would impair credit, increase taxation, deter immigration into the state, and halt capital investment.[24] The delegates could not complain that they had been left in any doubt about the seriousness of the situation nor that the provisional governor had failed to indicate the course of action which needed to be adopted.

On October 30 without either dissent or debate the secession ordinance of January 18, 1861 was repealed.[25] Although this was carried without a voice being raised in opposition, the continued belief in the states' rights idea of the continuing right to secede was evidenced by the fact that the original secession ordinance was repealed but not declared always to have been null and void. The fire and the fury of the earlier ordinance had burned itself out; its repeal took less than two minutes.[26] Even less time was taken over the question of the abolition of slavery. The wording of Article I, section 20, of the 1865 Constitution is, however, significant in that it indicates an acquiescence in *force majeure* rather than any fundamental belief in the desirability of abolition, and, secondly, the hope that some monetary compensation might eventually be secured from the government of the United States as had been the case with Britain's compensated emancipation policy in the West Indies.

The government of the United States having, as a war measure, proclaimed all slaves held or owned in this State emancipated from slavery, and having carried that proclamation into full practical effect, there shall henceforth be, within the State of Georgia, neither slavery nor involuntary servitude, save as a punishment for crime, after legal conviction thereof. *Provided*, this acquiescence in the action of the government of the United States is not intended to operate as a relinquishment, waiver or estoppel of such claim for compensation of loss sustained by reason of the emancipation of his slaves, as any citizen of Georgia may hereafter make upon the justice and magnanimity of that government.[27]

Georgia recognized the *fait accompli* without even a whisper of dissent and further resistance at this point was as feeble as the light from the flickering candle held in the hand of the clerk by which the clause was read and accepted.[28]

Another article charged the General Assembly at its next session with the duty of providing laws for the protection of the person and property of the free colored people and to prescribe safeguards for their legal rights.[29] One further article showed little equivocation, and

---

21 *Ibid.*

22 *Ibid.*, p. 237.

23 This seemingly conflicts with the report of the superintendent of the road given above, p. 38.

24 Candler, ed., IV, pp. 38ff.

25 *Journal of the Constitutional Convention, 1865*, pp. 17–18; *Joint Committee on Reconstruction*, III, p. 187.

26 Andrews, p. 243. In the interests of harmony, Joshua Hill did not take up his notice of motion for reconsideration to make secession null and void. It is perhaps indicative of the continued belief in states' rights that in the convention's address to Andrew Johnson before its adjournment, reference was made to the repeal of ordinances adopted with the purpose of separating themselves from the United States and entering into *another confederacy* (italics mine).

27 *Constitution of Georgia, 1865*, Article I, section 20.

28 Andrews, p. 247.

29 *Constitution of Georgia, 1865*, Article II, section 5.

that was the prohibition forever of marriage relations between white persons and persons of African descent. The assembly was again charged with the task of providing legislation for the punishment of any civil official or minister of the gospel who should knowingly perform such a marriage.[30] However far members of the convention were prepared to go regarding emancipation and laws for the protection of a freedman's person and property, there was no doubt in their minds that miscegenation was undesirable (whatever the situation had been before the war) and should be prevented by force of law. Interbreeding to provide interest on capital invested in a female slave was sound economically (and not physically distasteful), but interbreeding after emancipation could only lead to mongrelization and increased economic burdens on white Georgians.

The abolition of slavery and the repeal of the secession ordinance had been accepted without debate or division, but the question of the repudiation of the war debt occupied many hours of discussion and argument. Whether the incurment of the debt was justified or not was not the issue — repudiation was a matter of simple economics and self-interest. Although the provisional governor had stated that there was no legal or moral obligation to pay off the war debt and that it would have to be repudiated, it was estimated that less than a quarter of the delegates to the convention shared his views.[31] Those in favor of the assumption of the war debt made great play with the "integrity and honor of Georgia"[32] and with the duties they had to the starving orphans and widows of Confederate soldiers. The eyes of the delegates may well have been full of tears at such a harrowing prospect, but the state's coffers were empty of dollars and J. R. Parrott of Bartow county bluntly said that assuming the war debt would in fact be the means whereby those least able to afford it would be taxed to pay those who had speculated in state bonds on the home front while others went off to fight.[33] One interesting suggestion in the light of future events was that the Western and Atlantic Railroad, valued at some $10,000,000, should be sold and the purchasers incorporated. Shares at $100 each would be paid for in national currency at par, in Georgia bonds, issued before the war at ninety-five cents on the dollar and in the various bond issues constituting the war debt at rates ranging from twenty-five to seventy-five cents on the dollar. This highly ingenious and indirect method of paying off the war debt, behind which some members thought they could see the fine hand of ex-Governor Brown, was strongly opposed by Joshua Hill and finally tabled.[34]

Whichever way those in favor of assumption twisted and turned, however, there was no way around the clear and explicit statements to the provisional governor of President Andrew Johnson and his Secretary of State, William H. Seward, that Georgia would not be readmitted to the Union until every dollar of debt created for the purpose of aiding the rebellion against the government of the United States was repudiated.[35] The struggle continued until the close of the session, when the convention, recognizing that there was no alternative but to comply, passed by 135–117 votes an ordinance of repudiation, nullifying all debts created for the purpose of carrying on war against the United States.[36] The only solace for those opposed to repudiation was that the ordinance was not incorporated into the Constitution, which made it possible for subsequent legislatures, once Georgia was again in control of her own affairs, to reconsider the question of the payment of the war debts.[37] How far the members of the convention were personally and financially interested in this question and how much pressure was brought to bear on them behind the scenes will probably never be known in detail, but in an analysis of the voting the Augusta *Daily Constitutionalist* found that nearly half of the negative vote came from thirty-seven wealthy and well-populated counties, from judges, army men, lawyers, editors, doctors, and planters. Those in favor of repudiation came from more remote, sparsely-populated, and poorer districts that "by means of a faulty system, out vote three to one in legislative halls ten times their population and twenty times their wealth."[38] Hav-

---

30   *Ibid.*, Article V, section 1.

31   Andrews, p. 260.

32   These considerations did not weigh very heavily in the balance in 1872 when the "redeemers" repudiated the debts incurred by Governor Rufus Bullock and the Republicans.

33   Andrews, pp. 272–274.

34   *Ibid.*, p. 272.

35   Candler, ed., IV, pp. 50–51.

36   *Journal of the Constitutional Convention, 1865*, pp. 135–136.

37   One further loophole left the way open for the presentation of claims which could show quite clearly that the debts had been incurred for purposes completely removed from that of the prosecution of the war.

38   Augusta *Daily Constitutionalist*, November 15, 1865, quoted by Ethel K. Ware, *A Constitutional History of Georgia* (Columbia University Press, 1947), pp. 131–132. These words must have been repeated thousands of times almost to the

ing complied with President Johnson's prerequisites for readmission to the Union, the convention adjourned on November 8, 1865, subject to recall by its president. Before adjournment, however, the convention was able to clear the way for the election a week later of Judge Charles J. Jenkins to the governorship. Though Miss Thompson[39] gives the impression in her work that Judge Jenkins was very much an automatic choice, a great deal of maneuvering had taken place before his candidature was announced. Howell Cobb had written to his wife at the end of October 1865, "I understand that the race for Governor will be between that gentleman patriot and statesman, C. J. Jenkins and that impersonation of corruption and hypocrisy, Joe Brown. There can be no doubt about the result."[40] Alexander H. Stephens was urged to declare himself a candidate for governor on the grounds that more than any other man in the state he had the confidence of men both in the North and in the South. If he were unwilling to stand then he should go to Washington, preferably as one of the state's senators and, if not, as one of Georgia's representatives.[41]

On November 9 Brown wrote to Stephens, informing him that as he had not been able to secure Stephens's nomination for the governorship, he had given an ultimatum to Charles J. Jenkins that unless he was prepared to bury all past party differences and to make appointments to office without regard to party he, Brown, would run against him. This Jenkins agreed to do, although Brown assured Stephens that he would have preferred *him* to be governor. At the same time he offered Stephens his support for United States senator.[42] The extent of Brown's political power can be seen in another letter to Stephens written on November 14 in which he confidently asserted that had he known that Stephens would have accepted nomination for the governorship any time during the first week of the convention, "all opposition could have been silenced and you could have had a clear field." As this was now impossible, Brown felt certain that Stephens could be elected as a senator to Congress without any opposition.[43]

Seemingly Stephens had let his willingness to run be known to Judge O. A. Lochrane, but Lochrane for reasons best known to himself delayed for some days before revealing this information.[44] In the meanwhile, Jenkins was brought out to defeat Brown; had it been known in time that Stephens was prepared to run, both Brown and Jenkins would have withdrawn in his favor.[45] Jenkins himself assured Stephens of his regret that the information had not arrived in time, and hinted that it might have been suppressed deliberately. He concluded mournfully that although he had been in office barely two days, he was already besieged by hordes of men greedy for office.[46]

In the state elections of November 15, Jenkins was elected with an overwhelming majority, by 37,200 votes to fewer than 700 scattered among a dozen or so names.[47] The result reflected the acceptability of Jenkins to all sides in that he had been a staunch Unionist in 1861 but had gone with the state during the war. At the same time his position on the bench had enabled him to remain aloof and inactive. Yet in the recent convention he had gone on record as opposed to the repudiation of the war debt.[48]

In this election there were no disfranchised voters as had been the

---

present day by those opposed to Georgia's notorious "unit rule" by which rural counties outvoted the great urban centers like Atlanta in Fulton county.

39 Thompson, p. 153.

40 Cobb Collection, Cobb to his wife, October 28, 1865. The bitter hatred which existed between Cobb and Brown would seem to have become intensified in the last year of the war. At that time Cobb saw the desperate need for calling up the reserves and Brown's exemption certificates to thousands of state officials seemed to him completely unjustifiable. Cobb was convinced that Brown was also seizing the opportunity to speculate in land purchases in southwest Georgia while others were doing the fighting. Brown, denying all Cobb's interpretations and allegations, hit back with the accusation that Cobb had lived in ease upon his wife's property while creditors were kept waiting. Cobb's bitterness can be seen in the closing paragraph of one letter to Brown: "I shall leave you in your allusions to my own pecuniary embarrassments in the past to the full enjoyment of all the pleasure which a low and groveling mind derives from the repetition of stale and malicious slanders. When those who originated them blush in the remembrance of their turpitude, the subject becomes eminently suited to one of your taste and instincts." *Official Records*, Series IV, Vol. III, pp. 347–349, 417–422, 431–439, 442–444.

41 Alexander H. Stephens Papers, Crawford to Stephens, October 6, 1865; Parrott to Stephens, November 5, 1865.

42 *Ibid.*, Brown to Stephens, November 9, 1865.

43 *Ibid.*, Brown to Stephens, November 14, 1865.

44 Lochrane succeeded Brown as chief-justice of the Supreme Court of Georgia in 1870.

45 Alexander H. Stephens Papers, J. B. Dumble to Stephens, November 17, 1865.

46 *Ibid.*, Jenkins to Stephens, November 17, 1865. Jenkins may have been pointing the finger of suspicion at Brown because Brown subsequently became a partner of Lochrane and the notorious carpetbag financier, Hannibal I. Kimball, in a law firm. Louise B. Hill, *Joseph E. Brown and the Confederacy* (Chapel Hill, 1930), p. 288. It is, of course, quite possible that A. H. Stephens was being very skillfully shunted off onto a political siding.

47 *Georgia House Journal, 1865*, p. 17.

48 Andrews, pp. 280, 326.

case for the convention; this was reflected in the composition of the new legislature, where Unionists and anti-secessionists were less in evidence. The electorate returned a high proportion of ex-Confederates with good military records, and in a sense foreshadowed the Northern postwar political tactics of "waving the bloody shirt." Undoubtedly this legislature reflected more clearly than the convention the feelings of Georgians, but whether they were men of superior ability, as Miss Thompson asserts,[49] is a matter for debate. At this stage, Joseph E. Brown was among the few secessionists with sufficient political acumen to recognize the need for cooperation with the federal government, at least for the moment; he was prepared to forego threadbare patriotic gestures in exchange for the positive benefits of swift readmission to the Union.[50]

The first meeting of the legislature took place at Milledgeville on December 4, 1865, and the election to Congress of Alexander H. Stephens, former vice-president of the Confederacy,[51] and Herschel V. Johnson, a former senator of the Confederacy, was indicative of the feelings of the state legislature. The desire to send able men as Georgia's representatives to the United States Senate was a worthy one, but at the same time it showed a woeful lack of understanding of how far the North would tolerate the return to power of former prominent Confederates. Though admittedly neither Stephens nor Johnson had been rabid secessionists, no one would claim that they had been nonentities during the war.[52] Greater discretion would have been shown had men like Joshua Hill or provisional governor Johnson been elected. Even less auspicious was the election of the seven Georgia representatives to the United States House of Representatives, not one of whom could take the Test Oath and who, for the most part, although not original secessionists, had risen to high rank in the Confederate armies and who did not play down their records of war service.[53] It is difficult to understand what Georgia hoped to achieve by sending prominent Confederates to Congress. Many of those in positions of leadership must have been aware that President Johnson's *fait accompli* reconstruction was likely to come under heavy attack from the radical wing of the Republican party in the North once Congress reassembled at the beginning of December 1865. If it were a gesture of the justifiable pride which Georgians had in the part they had played during the war, then it was misplaced. It would have been far more statesmanlike to have kept their pride in their pocket and taken it out for burnishing when circumstances were more propitious and the consequences of such a demonstration less painful. Howell Cobb, at least, seemed to be under no illusions about the attitude of Congress. Early in December he wrote to his wife,

If the movements of Sumner in the Senate and Thad Stevens in the House foreshadow the future policy of the Government, then indeed are our darkest days yet to come . . . They . . . propose to deal severely with J. Davis [Jefferson Davis, president of the Confederacy], Toombs and myself and others for treachery . . . and someone moved to venture to add the names of Buchanan [ex-President James Buchanan] and Breckenridge [John C. Breckenridge of Kentucky, Buchanan's pro-slavery Vice-President]. What will old Buck say when he finds himself as prominently associated with the leading rebels.[54]

---

49   Thompson, p. 153.

50   Louise B. Hill, Brown's biographer, is somewhat harsh on him when suggesting (pp. 326–327) that because he feared the confiscation of his property, his moral courage gave way and he advocated cooperation with the government and subsequently threw in his lot with the Radical Republicans until it was safe to return to the Democratic party.

51   Andrews, p. 358, described him at this time as "a little old man with most marvellous eyes, looking not so much like a human being as like a character from one of Dickens' stories."

52   As early as November 24, Andrew Johnson had telegraphed General Steedman at Augusta to the effect that however much he, personally, respected Stephens, the latter would be quite unacceptable as a senator from Georgia to the United States Senate. *Official Records*, Series II, Vol. VIII, p. 818. Many years later a tribute to Stephens's standing in Georgia at this time came from a most unexpected quarter, from ex-Governor Rufus B. Bullock, to many the personification of all that was bad in Radical Reconstruction. He wrote that Stephens was "the fittest and safest man for the position at that time. He commanded the unlimited confidence of the Union element — the anti-secession sentiment of Georgia, which, before hostilities were inaugurated, constituted a majority. The intelligence and property of Georgia were not in favor of the experiment of secession . . . and Mr. Stephens was their leader." Rufus B. Bullock, "Reconstruction in Georgia," *Independent*, March 19, 1903, p. 670.

53   Miss Thompson (p. 155) describes them as "moderate men" although Andrews (pp. 326–330) hardly bears out this description of them and particularly not in the case of Colonel James D. Matthews of Oglethorpe county whom he described as "the most uncompromising malcontent in the Congressional delegation," "one of the worst Rebels in the district," and "as badly disposed toward the government and the new order of things as any man I have met in all my tour" (p. 354). It is a pity in some ways that Matthews was unable to take his seat, because he was exactly the sort of man Thaddeus Stevens would have enjoyed flaying with his invective.

54   Cobb Collection, Cobb to his wife, December 7, 1865. Jenkins, however, had high hopes of Georgia's being soon represented in Congress. Candler, ed., IV, pp. 448–449.

Toombs, who had no doubts about his fate, should he be captured, prudently had left the country. He wrote from Havana expressing some regret that Stephens was prepared to return to Congress but very little about anything else.

I should certainly have been imprisoned and treated with indignity by our beloved brethren of the North . . . I see nothing in the conduct of President Johnson to approve — not a single act . . . except Sumner wants him to order the white slaves of the South to admit the black ones to suffrage. . . . For . . . the Johnsons, Browns etc. in Georgia, I have a contempt that no language can measure. They seem to glory in their shame and revel in the ruin and degradation of those whom they pretend to serve . . .[55]

The election of senators and representatives to Congress was but part of the picture. The legislature was faced with the task of implementing in Georgia the provisions of Andrew Johnson's plan of reconstruction. An immediate necessity was that of ratifying the Thirteenth Amendment to the Constitution of the United States. Whatever residual reluctance there may have been to recognize that emancipation was a fact, there was little if anything to be gained by refusing to ratify. Provisional governor Johnson stated in a message to the legislature that Georgia could not revive slavery even if she wished, but he was rather over-optimistic in asserting that "the ratification of this amendment . . . will remove from among us that cause of bitterness and sectional strife which has wasted our property and deluged our land in blood."[56] The legislature did make a halfhearted attempt to add a rider to the effect that Congress had only the power to make permanent the emancipation of the slaves, and that the state alone could confer the rights of citizenship. This failed and the final declaration of emancipation was made on December 5–6.[57] On December 14, Jenkins was inaugurated as governor and in his inaugural address called for legislation to safeguard the rights of the freedmen. He maintained that the Negro in bondage had been raised immeasurably above the contemporary African by a system which had lightly taxed his physical energies and supplied all his needs from the cradle to the grave. He reminded the legislators that during the war the slaves had remained staunchly loyal and since obtaining their freedom had behaved extremely well; their rights of person and property, however, would have to be made perfectly secure. To achieve this the courts must be open to them and the testimony of their own race must be admitted in both civil and criminal cases. He warned the legislators, and the Negroes indirectly, that the latter would have to be guarded against "the fatal delusion of social and political equality" and urged that "the necessity of subordination and dependence should be riveted on their convictions."[58]

Ex-Governor Brown was approached for his views on the subject by members of the legislature, and in February 1866 he published the substance of his advice in the press.[59] He stressed that the slaves were now free and must have equal rights with whites, however mortifying this might be to white Southerners. He did not personally believe that God had made Negroes equal to white people either intellectually or socially, "and unless madness rules the hour, they will never be placed upon a basis of political equality with us . . . they are not competent to the task of self-government, much less to aid in governing a great nation of white people." Nevertheless, he believed that although the Negro should not be allowed to sit on juries or be given the right to vote, it was imperative that he should have equal legal rights to sue and be sued and to testify in all the courts of the state. He should be subject to the same penalties as the white man and have the same lawful guarantee of life, liberty, and property. Only in this way could interference from the Freedmen's Bureau be avoided.[60]

As a result of this kind of sound advice the Georgia legislature refrained from passing a "black code" of laws for the regulation of the freedmen as such other Southern states as Mississippi had. Negroes[61] were given the right to sue and be sued; to make and enforce contracts; to be parties to agreements and give evidence; to inherit, purchase, lease, sell, hold, and convey real and personal property; to have full benefit of all laws for the security of persons and estate; and to be free from subjection to any different pain or penalty for the commission of any act or offense than those prescribed for white persons. The penal

---

55   Alexander H. Stephens Papers, Toombs to Stephens, December 15, 1865.
56   *Georgia Senate Journal, 1865*, p. 14.
57   *Ibid.*, p. 9.
58   *Ibid.*, pp. 64–65.
59   Atlanta *Daily Intelligencer*, February 18, 1866, Brown scrapbooks, and Townsend Collection, Vol. 65, no. 131.
60   For further views of white–Negro relations see below, pp. 61ff.
61   Persons of color were defined as all Negroes, mulattoes, mestizoes, and their descendants having one eighth Negro or African blood.

code was altered so as to impose the death penalty for burglary in the night, horse-stealing, rape, and arson.[62] Several hundred crimes including all species of larceny (except the above) were made misdemeanors punishable by whipping, imprisonment, or fine. This reduction from felonies to misdemeanors was done out of consideration for the ignorance of the freedmen which would have made the severer penalties imposed by earlier laws unjust if applied to them. Heretofore the only law they had had to obey was the will of their masters. Now they were subject to a complex of laws about which they knew virtually nothing. Until they understood their responsibilities as well as their rights under the law, failure to apply the laws intelligently could have resulted in half the Negro population's being subject to severe penalties for crimes unwittingly committed. Vagrancy, apprentice, and enticement laws were also passed on a noncolor basis; intermarriage of the races was prohibited; slave marriages were validated and their issue legitimized.[63]

Although the laws of Georgia compared favorably, at least on the surface, with those of other states, they were primarily designed to deal effectively with the social realities of the times. The apprentice law which bound out orphaned minors until they reached twenty-one had so many loopholes for the master to evade the statutory requirements that, at the age of twenty-one, an apprentice could well find himself in the position of having to take court action to obtain even the minimum $100 allowance laid down by law for his services. Even more dangerous in its implications was the vagrancy law, whereby a vagrant, at the discretion of the court, might be fined or imprisoned or sentenced to hard labor on the public works for not more than a year or bound out to some person "upon such valuable consideration as the court might prescribe." By these two laws, if they were not implemented strictly and impartially, the opportunity was provided for unscrupulous men to obtain bond servants at almost nominal cost. Although these laws technically were applicable to whites as well as colored people, the probability was that orphaned minors and vagrants would prove to be more numerous among colored people than among whites, especially when vagrancy could be given a very broad interpretation in an all-white court.[64]

By legislation such as this the position decreed for the Negro was one of political oblivion, social inferiority, and superficial legal equality. Legal equality was entirely dependent upon the good will and the genuine desire of the lawmakers and law enforcers to provide equality of treatment before the law, and the Southern lawgiver has not always been the most liberal and well-meaning of men when Negroes have become involved with the law. Superficially, therefore, Georgia could point to laws on the statute books which applied equally to white and colored citizens, laws which did not discriminate explicitly against the Negro. It was asking too much to expect that shrewd Northern lawyers would not recognize the implications of the laws of Georgia [65] or fail to recognize that the good will necessary to make equality before the law a reality was hardly likely to be widespread.[66] Those Northerners who expected that fraternal good feelings toward the Negro would be shown by Georgians would be disappointed and swiftly disillusioned.

One of the major reasons for the secession of the Southern states from the Union had been to preserve slavery — not because slavery was necessarily good, but because the alternative, the granting to Negroes of the same rights, even in part, as those enjoyed by whites, was undesirable. Slavery was the simplest, most effective method of regulating relations between white and black and for that reason alone was worth preserving. Opposition from Union elements in Georgia to secession came not because the Unionists necessarily doubted the constitutional right of the state to secede, but because they considered it inexpedient. Four years of war had proved them right. The South lacked the physical strength and resources successfully to break away. It proved nothing more. This was as much as many Georgians were prepared to concede after Appomattox. Little else had changed, and as far as the Negro was concerned, the fundamental reason for secession remained unchanged.

---

62   These crimes of which Negroes were generally accused had previously carried a maximum penalty of twenty years' imprisonment, except horse-stealing, previously set at five years' imprisonment. The death penalty could be commuted to life imprisonment.

63   *Acts of the General Assembly,* 1865–1866, pp. 234–235, 239–241.

64   Under the slave system children born to colored women were the responsibility of the slaveowner and not of the father. After the war, with the legalization of marriage between former slaves, children became the responsibility of their parents, and the acceptance of this responsibility was not always easy, especially should the parents be in financial difficulties.

65   Miss Thompson (p. 159), however, quotes favorable comments on Georgia's code of laws from the New York *Times.*

66   E. B. Adams of the American Union Commission maintained that Georgians were indifferent to the protection of the Negro and caustically commented, "They bury him when dead not, however, for respect to his person but to remove the nuisance." *De Bow's Review* (After the War Series), Vol. I, p. 550.

Though hostilities on the battlefields had ceased, the war continued on the constitutional, legislative, and social fronts. The conviction that each state had the right to decide the position to be occupied by the Negroes in that state, free from federal interference, was as strong as ever. By the beginning of 1866 Georgia had gone as far as she was prepared to go without compulsion to meet the conditions laid down for readmission to the Union — any concessions beyond those granted by then to the Negroes would be vigorously opposed and would nullify whatever advantages were to be gained by readmission. Georgians were prepared to be loyal citizens of the United States once more, but not at any price. Unenthusiastically but realistically they were prepared to accept Johnsonian reconstruction. Ex-Governor Brown's advice to cooperate and not to stand emotionally uncompromising amidst the ashes of a lost cause was sound although a little inconsistent to some. The editor of the Turnwold *Countryman* sardonically commented, "We see in the papers that Howell Cobb and Joseph E. Brown speak in glowing terms of our 'glorious future.' Now, if we are going to have such a glorious future with the abolition of slavery why did Cobb and Brown plunge us into such a bloody war to attain this abolition when we might have had it without any war at all?"[67] The *Countryman's* complaint basically was not so much against the policy that Brown was advocating as against Brown's advocacy. Such criticism could not be leveled against Alexander H. Stephens, who in an address before the Georgia house and senate in February 1866 took up a position close to that of Brown. He urged the members of the legislature to be patient, to forget the bitterness of the war years, and to put their trust in the President's restoration policy. With regard to the freedmen he advocated that as the weaker race they would have to be protected and granted equality before the law in the possession of all rights of person, liberty, and property, and that adequate education would have to be made available to them.[68] He was prepared to recognize property and education as qualifications for a limited form of suffrage, but his views on the Negro and his qualities in general bear a striking similarity to those of Joseph E. Brown.[69] "Equality does not exist between blacks and whites. The one race is by nature inferior in many respects, physically and mentally to the other . . . It is useless to war against the decrees of nature in attempting to make things equal which the Creator has made unequal." Two months later, he was able to assure the Joint Committee on Reconstruction [70] that an overwhelming majority of the people of Georgia were eager for the restoration of government, for her senators and representatives to take their places in Congress, and for Georgia to enjoy all her rights as a state of the Union under the amended Constitution of the United States. He left the committee in no doubt, however, that although he personally was prepared to consider some limited form of suffrage for the Negroes, the same majority of Georgians were utterly opposed to granting them the suffrage generally, and would view such a step as a major political disaster. They were equally opposed to any final attempt to exclude the Negro from the basis of representation. Their case was based on the belief that suffrage was exclusively a state matter and outside the jurisdiction of Congress to make it a condition of precedence to admission to the Union.[71]

The Report of the Joint Committee is a vast quarry of information, misinformation, and divergent views genuinely held. The main points of inquiry regarded the loyalty of Southerners (although what yardstick was used to measure loyalty is not clear) and the treatment of former slaves. Testimony not unnaturally varied and at times was so contradictory as to make it difficult to realize that witnesses were speaking of the same state. Major-General Edward Hatch of Iowa, for example, testified that Georgians were so bitter against the Union that it was impossible for Northern men to live there except under military protection and that the position of loyal Unionists there was even more precarious.[72] On the other hand, Brigadier-General John Tarbell, although considered a "Black Republican Yankee," encountered no overt hostility nor lack of courtesy. He was convinced that Georgians were eager to secure Northern capital to help restore the

---

67 February 13, 1866. The inclusion of Howell Cobb in this censure was somewhat unjust as Cobb was largely avoiding politics at this time in favor of rehabilitating his plantations.

68 *Georgia Senate Journal, 1865*, pp. 393, 395, 400–401.

69 Myrta L. Avary, ed., *Recollections of Alexander H. Stephens* (New York, 1910), pp. 207, 269–270, 517. For Brown's views see above, p. 55.

70 This Joint Committee of Congress was charged with the task of examining conditions in the Southern states and particularly the situation of the freedmen. Its report gave the *coup de grâce* to Johnsonian reconstruction and provided the basis for Radical Reconstruction.

71 *Report of the Joint Committee on Reconstruction* (Washington, 1866), pt. III, pp. 158–162.

72 *Ibid.*, pp. 7–8.

state, and Northern men were equally welcome. At the same time he warned the committee that there was a tendency in the North to over-rate the character and capacity for future improvement of the plantation Negro, and that those who were expecting a swift transformation from passive slave to active citizen were likely to be bitterly disappointed.[73] It was perhaps unfortunate that in the minds of some members of the committee there seemed to be direct correlation between loyalty to the Union and the treatment of Negroes. This equation of constitutional convictions and social attitudes created substantial misgivings on the one hand and incredulous bewilderment on the other. On such a basis as this, especially when complicated by the quarrel between Johnson and Congress over executive or legislative reconstruction, little could be expected at this time except that Georgia and the other Southern states would be left neither in nor out of the Union.

The problem of the Negro began to loom increasingly large. His con-stitutional and legal position seemed to most Georgians to have been quite satisfactorily settled. His social and economic position was a question which every Georgian, individually, would have to face.

---

73   *Ibid.*, pp. 156–157.

IV

GEORGIA'S BLACK LEGACY

THE proclamation to free niggers had only reduced prices for niggers. White trash who had never had a thousand dollars or fifteen hundred dollars to pay for a slave could get niggers now for a few dollars a head by giving them an advance against wages. Times change and new ways of getting slaves are cunningly devised.[1]

Black-White Relationships

IN GEORGIA, as in all the Southern states with a heavy Negro population, the question of the position of the colored people after the war was of critical importance. In 1860 Georgia had a population of 591,588 whites (80 per cent of whom were native-born Georgians), 425,298 blacks and 36,900 mulattoes as slaves, and 3,500 free colored people.[2] There was thus a fairly even balance of population between white and black, a balance which could only be viewed uneasily by white Georgians as the imminence of effective emancipation became greater with the end of the war. Only a madman could seriously consider the possibility of colonizing such numbers in Africa even if the colored population as free men and women were willing to take part in such an enterprise. Such a measure would, in any case, have paralyzed the economic life of Georgia. White Georgians needed their former slaves more than

---

1   John L. Spivak, *Georgia Nigger* (New York, 1932), pp. 138–139.
2   *U.S. Census, 1860,* "Population," pp. 72, 76.

they needed white Georgians. Garrison Frazier, the spokesman of a group of free-born and emancipated Negroes who met with E. M. Stanton and General Sherman in January 1865, maintained that the Negroes would rather live to themselves if possible because the prejudice against them in the South was such that it would take years to eradicate.[3] Frazier was being almost as unrealistic as the would-be colonizers. For better or for worse, whites and blacks were joined together by bonds much stronger than those of holy matrimony — economic survival. The bonds might chafe both, but a divorce was out of the question.

Yet for some slavery died hard in Georgia, not necessarily because they considered slavery the best of all possible systems, but because with emancipation the white Southerner for the first time faced the reality of having to live in a society where the black man could claim, even if he did not get, political and social equality. Hitherto, the comparatively small number of free Negroes and the subordinate position in society to which they had been relegated had not been a threat in any way to white supremacy. Even though the end of the war may have brought relief from the moral stigma of slavery, it presented white Georgians with more immediate and more complex problems.

Most Georgians would seem to have accepted abolition as a fact even if they did not accept it with very good grace, but there were diehards who were quick to see the opportunity for legal sleight of hand which would give the federal government the shadow of emancipation and Georgia the substance of slavery. General John T. Morgan, a white supremacist from Alabama, while in southwest Georgia, urged that, as the Constitution of the United States gave the power to inflict involuntary servitude as a punishment for crime, a suitable law should be framed by the state jurists which would enable them to sell into bondage once more those Negroes found guilty of certain crimes. He was quite sure that, in conjunction with the whipping post and the pillory, this would do more to check vagrancy, theft, robbery, and other crimes than all the penitentiaries that could be built.[4] That a resort would be made to backdoor methods was realized by a Unionist in the same part of the state in October 1865. He maintained that "If legal chicanery can avail, those rights [of the Negro] will be but nominal and they will remain as they have ever been, isolated and apart — free in name but slaves in fact."[5] The freedman himself was often in some doubt as to his standing; Clara Barton of Massachusetts, the American Florence Nightingale, testified before the Joint Committee on Reconstruction that when she arrived at Andersonville she encountered Negroes there who believed that, with the death of Lincoln, they had become slaves once more.[6] Some planters obviously were in no hurry to enlighten their former slaves as to their new status, clinging to the hope that despite the Emancipation Proclamation, the outcome of the war, and the Thirteenth Amendment to the Constitution, the institution of slavery might be continued in some modified form.[7]

According to a correspondent of the New York *Times* writing from Milledgeville in November 1865, opposition to the Negro came for the most part not from former slaveholders but from "ex–nigger drivers, ex–nigger traders, ex–nigger whippers or representatives of that portion of communities known as the 'poor whites' — slaves with white faces."[8] Hatred, fear, resentment, and distrust of the Negro, in their many forms, came, however, from all quarters and from all sections of society. The colored man was despised, and anyone sympathizing with him rapidly discovered that he was *persona non grata* in his own community.[9] Social ostracism, when ruthlessly and uncompromisingly put into action, rapidly dried up the wellsprings of overt sympathy and many may well have overstressed their antipathy to the Negro in order to ensure their own social acceptability. Toombs, the unrepentant, unreconstructed rebel was never at any time mealymouthed in his attitude, "They are of the human race but they are not of my race. They are a lower order of human beings."[10] And again, later, "as long as the African and Caucasian races co-exist in the same society, the subordination of the African is the necessary, proper and normal condition . . . calculated to pro-

---

3   "Colloquy with Colored Ministers," *Journal of Negro History*, XVI (1931), pp. 88–94, *Official Records*, Series I, Vol. XLVII, pt. 2, pp. 37–41.

4   Andrews, pp. 324, 371. See also *Nation*, October 5, 1865.

5   New York *Evening Post*, November 9, 1865. See also Schurz, Senate Ex. Doc. no. 2, 39 Cong., 1 sess., Vol. I, Doc. no. 44, p. 105.

6   *Report of the Joint Committee on Reconstruction*, pt. III, p. 103.

7   P. S. Flippin, *Herschel V. Johnson* (Richmond, 1931), p. 264. For confirmatory evidence see the testimony of Major-General Rufus Saxton and H. S. Welles of the Brunswick and Florida Railroad Company, *Report of the Joint Committee on Reconstruction*, pt. III, pp. 100, 109–110.

8   New York *Times*, November 23, 1865.

9   *National Freedman*, I, no. 8, pp. 254–255.

10   Atlanta *Constitution*, August 29, 1877.

mote the highest interest and greatest happiness of both races."[11] An-other Georgian, in Americus, delivered himself of the delightfully blood-thirsty sentiment that "Hell's the place for Yankees and I want 'em all to go thar as soon's possible and take the niggers 'long with 'em."[12] His feelings were drawn out from the bitterness of defeat but he was not alone. Martin J. Crawford, writing to Mrs. Howell Cobb in November 1865, was equally bitter, "I was sorry to hear that the small-pox had broken out in Athens . . . as for the Negroes I don't care how many of them have it — so they die. It is a *real luxury* now to know that they are shuffling off their thieving coils."[13] Hatred of the Negro was blended with a long-held fear of Negro insurrection and the exaction of payment in blood for the long years of slavery. Eliza Frances Andrews was afraid that with the training in arms that they had received from the Northern armies, the Negroes would re-enact the roles of the sepoys in the In-dian Mutiny.[14]

A race war is sure to come sooner or later and we shall have only the Yankees to thank for it . . . No power on earth can raise an inferior, savage race above their civilized masters and keep them there . . . Eventually the negro race will either be exterminated or reduced to some system of apprenticeship embodying the best features of slavery, but this generation will not live to see it.[15]

Similar sentiments were expressed by the Macon *Telegraph*, which dolorously warned its readers that "the scenes of bloodshed and massa-cre of St. Domingo will be re-enacted in our midst before the close of the year."[16]

Of necessity, individual attitudes ranged widely, from a pathological hatred of the colored people to a kindly yet guarded tolerance of these social outsiders. Though the latter attitude was not uncommon, it could vary, depending upon how far the freedmen were prepared to accept the immutability of their inferior position. Any assault upon the citadel of white supremacy could bring an instinctive violent reaction, not so much on a personal basis but against the race generally.

One correspondent of Howell Cobb was convinced that freedom had had a decidedly injurious effect upon the moral character of the Negro [17] and that the juxtaposition of two distinct races in a state of freedom was *ipso facto* evil; "The blacks are ever envious of the superiority of the whites and clamorous for equality while using every means to appro-priate their property: and the whites are inspired with contempt for the blacks and constantly irritated and provoked by their bad conduct."[18]

The concern of many white Georgians with the moral welfare of the Negro was partly genuine and partly an unconscious resentment lest, in addition to his physical freedom, the Negro should retain a moral freedom over and above that enjoyed by whites, restricted as they increasingly were by the social mores of the times. The planter's wife who had had to accept her husband's right to have intercourse with a slave woman could no longer tolerate an association which was now, under freedom, strictly adulterous. The sudden change of the slave's coffle for the freedman's marriage ring undoubtedly appeared to be both puzzling and ironic to many Negroes. At one meeting of the Meth-

---

11 *Ibid.*, December 10, 1885. Even the devout Moravian missionary Elizabeth Sterchi, had little patience with anything that smacked of equality: "the posterity of Ham has been cursed and shall remain at the place where the Lord has placed it . . . the black race cannot be placed on a level with the white one: men cannot undo what God has done." Adelaide L. Fries, "The Elizabeth Sterchi Letters," *Atlanta Historical Bulletin*, V (1940), p. 103.

12 Andrews, p. 320.

13 Cobb Collection, Crawford to Mrs. Cobb, November 3, 1865. One estimate was that by the end of June 1865 some 5,000 Negroes had already died and mortality rates seemed to be rising. R. N. Gourdin Papers, E. C. Anderson letter, June 26, 1865.

14 The speed with which white troops were demobilized from the Northern armies once the war was over increased dependence upon colored troops for garrison duties in the Southern states. Southerners bitterly resented defeat, but even more bitterly did they resent the presence of Negroes in uniform, with arms in their hands and in a position to exercise authority. The presence of colored troops in Georgia inevitably inflamed reactions to actual or imagined insults offered to white Georgians. In February 1866 it was decided to send a commissioner to Washington to protest strongly against the presence of Negro troops and the placing of "our former slaves with arms in their hands, to arrest, fine or imprison . . . to maltreat our citizens and insult their wives and daughters." The necessity to maintain troops in the state was recognized, but such troops had to be white men under competent officers. *Georgia Senate Journal, 1865*, pp. 856–857.

15 King, pp. 315–316.

16 July 16, 1865, quoted by New York *World*, July 27, 1865.

17 Frances Butler Leigh, *Ten Years on a Georgia Plantation* (London, 1883), p. 238, found that after a few years of freedom Negro women were rarely chaste. So many factors, however, have to be considered in this context that the views of Mrs. Leigh cannot be given very much weight. In fact, she recanted quite explicitly when she wrote in the above edition (p. 4), "I copy my impressions of things as they struck me then, although in many cases later events proved how false these impressions were and how often mistaken I was in the opinions I formed." This acknowledgment of error has been ignored by many Southern historians, who prefer to quote at length her first impressions.

18 Phillips, ed., Josephus Anderson to Howell Cobb, September 8, 1866.

odist Conference of Georgia it was resolved "that marriage irrespective of color is a good thing"; the resolution urged the adoption of a law which should secure protection for the slaves but not interfere with the legal rights of the slaveowner.[19] To put such a camel of contradictions through a legislative needle's eye would have been a matter of some difficulty; a not untypical reaction to a similar suggestion made by Dr. N. M. Crawford of Mercer was shown by the editor of the Turnwold *Countryman*; such a measure he considered tantamount to abolition and suggested: "*If he can* let him confer upon them the sanctity of the marriage relation: let him make them all virtuous and chaste and continent: let him teach them to read the Bible and Shakspeare and then let him confer upon them liberty and a white skin."[20] Robert Toombs, as blunt as ever, expressed much the same sentiments; more briefly but more pungently, "Now what does the Negro know about the obligations of the marriage relation? No more, sir, than the parish bull or the village heifer."[21] Moralizing and good advice were more common than good works. The Reverend Elias Yulee, for instance, published a long homily to the colored people which was doubtless considered sound advice by most Georgians. He warned the Negroes strongly against being taken in by old-line abolitionists who were mistakenly encouraging them to assert their independence of and equality with the whites. These were obviously impossible aspirations on the part of the colored people, because experience had shown quite clearly that intellectually they could not compete with the white man. Had they remained in Africa they would still be living in a state of degrading barbarism. New Englanders had brought them to America as slaves, but fortunately for them Georgians had seen fit to raise them up from their savagery.[22] Their future in America could only be assured if they were willing to continue as freedmen in the same subservient position as when they were slaves. He warned them that "If he [the Negro] attempts to introduce a new *Africa* in the South, his days are numbered and civilization will sweep him out of its track. The race can only live in, by and through the white race."[23] There were those, of course, who were quite prepared to do their share in expediting the demise of the colored people. The Savannah correspondent of the New York *Herald* maintained that "the shooting or stringing up of some obstreperous 'nigger' by the Regulators is so common an occurrence as to excite little remark."[24] In July 1866 it was reported that at Toomsboro, Wilkinson county, two to three hundred people took from jail a Negro called Pompey O'Bannon who was accused of the murder of a white woman. They chained him to a tree, cut his ears off, forced Negroes to pile faggots around him, burned him to death, and then threw his body to the dogs.[25] The later Ku-Klux Klan thus brought nothing new into being; it simply provided the means and the organization for a collective expression of racial antipathy which individuals as individuals could only express less effectively.

A more serious problem than that of the danger of lynching or being murdered faced Negroes who left the the plantations to congregate in or about the towns and cities of the state; that was the high mortality from sickness, disease, and destitution. The irony was that in seeking greater security in the towns under the protection of Federal officers, the Negro was exposed to added danger from the urban squalor in which he was forced to live. Too often, Negroes found it impossible to rent any form of housing except primitive outbuildings. Reasonable accommodation could not be had firstly because they could not afford to pay the rents asked and secondly because a white owner of property would not rent a house to a Negro, as he knew full well that afterwards he would never be able to rent it again to a white person. The result was that those places which could be rented were terribly overcrowded. A correspondent of the New York *World* at Washington, Georgia, wrote, "I have passed places inhabited by crowds of freedmen where in hot summer weather the stench was so great that I had to stop up my nose and cross to the other side of the street."[26] Squalor, dirt, and ignorance gave rise to disease and ill health; by Christmas 1865 severe outbreaks of smallpox occurred among Negroes living at Augusta, Macon, Milledgeville, and other parts of the state.[27] Where on the plantations the health of the slave had been fairly good and medical attention had

---

19   *Central Presbyterian,* January 21, 1865, in Townsend Collection, Vol. 53, no. 419.

20   April 18, 1865.

21   Atlanta *Constitution,* November 5, 1871.

22   Elias Yulee, *An Address to the Colored People of Georgia* (Savannah, Republican job office, 1868), pp. 6–9.

23   *Ibid.,* p. 15.

24   December 20, 1865, Townsend Collection, Vol. 63, no. 211. The "regulators," "jayhawkers," and "black-horse cavalry" were early groups of poor-white thugs, who enjoyed the opportunity now provided to kill, maim, or terrorize the Negro.

25   Townsend Collection, Vol. 67, no. 152.

26   October 7, 1865.

27   *Ibid.,* December 26, 1865; W. S. Thomson Papers, December 7, 1865.